Dr. Bob Smart sounds his ca  a
process that awakens the Cl ,
to see death as gain, and to ı ɔ
not have to surrender to th ıl
insight and compassion he described the p n
of God's grace can move such a calling from potential to reality. Bob Smart is a
true doctor of souls, describing the strengths and weaknesses of each phase of
Christian maturity with such pastoral precision that we are able to activate the
best and avoid the worst of Christian intentionality for the sake of Christ.

-Bryan Chapell
Pastor Grace Presbyterian Church

In *Intentionality for Christ* Dr. Bob Smart once again guides us on our path to
spiritual maturity with wisdom and grace. Because he writes of what he has
learned from his own walk with the Lord who daily leads him, his readers can
trust his God-given counsel. For my part, I will be eternally grateful that during
my midlife years, God saw fit to allow me to sit under Dr. Smart's teaching. His
impact on that season of my life reverberates today. I pray his readers will find
in this book the treasure that is there to be mined: a life lived intentionally for
the glory of Christ.

-Becky Shamess
Founding Head of School
Cornerstone Christian Academy
Bloomington, IL

Intentionality for Christ, serves as a wakeup call for slumbering Christians, who
find themselves asleep at the wheel aimlessly living without meaning purpose
or joy. In a world full of options and distractions it is easy to become hypnotized
into a nothingness existence. The good news is that it is not too late. In his short
inspiring and very practical book Bob Smart rouses a generation of believers,
not with harsh condemnation but with the sweet aroma of "more". Not the "God
wants more *from* you" kind of more, but the "God has so much more *for* you"
and that more is found in the joy of intentionally living "for Christ not for self",
"for His glory not our own" and "by His strength and not our own." For those

brave enough to take the first steps so much "more" awaits in learning to live intentionally for Christ.

-Pastor Adrian C. Das

Pastor Westminster Presbyterian Church (PCA) Godfrey, Illinois

You may be tempted as you begin reading *Intentionality for Christ: What's My Aim?*, the third book in Dr. Robert Smart's four book series on Spiritual Formation, to stop because the concept of spiritual formation seems a bit foreign and complicated. Don't do it! Read on. And also read the first two books in the series. In book 3, Dr. Bob masterfully addresses spiritual formation in a comprehensive, thought-provoking, delightful, and practical manner. Comprehensive as he weaves together all the elements and enemies of spiritual formation. Thought-provoking as he reasons why spiritual formation must demand our total attention and effort. Delightful as he brings in personal examples of failure and renewed commitment to try again. And practical as he carefully designs the steps and the fill-in-the-blank templates for our follow-through as we get serious about spiritual formation.

As you read *Intentionality for Christ,* you cannot help but be challenged and convinced by Dr. Bob's passion for spiritual formation, both in his own life and in the life of others as he has personally taken many friends and church members through the quest for seeing Christ formed in our lives. Bob echoes Paul's words Galatians 4:19, "I am again in anguish of childbirth until Christ is formed in you." You will come away from reading *Intentionality for Christ* with a passion to see Christ formed in you and others whom you love. But even more importantly, you will know how to go about seeing Christ formed in you.

-Rev. L. William Hesterberg, Th.M.

President of International Theological Educational Ministries (ITEM)

Intentionality For Christ

WHAT'S MY AIM?

ROBERT DAVIS SMART

WESTBOW
PRESS®
A DIVISION OF THOMAS NELSON
& ZONDERVAN

WestBow Press books may be ordered through booksellers or by contacting:

WestBow Press
A Division of Thomas Nelson & Zondervan
1663 Liberty Drive
Bloomington, IN 47403
www.westbowpress.com
1 (866) 928-1240

The Holy Bible, English Standard Version® (ESV®) Copyright © 2001 by Crossway, a publishing ministry of Good News Publishers, 1300 Crescent Street, Wheaton, Illinois 60187, USA. All rights reserved. ESV® Text Edition: 2016

Interior Graphics/Art Credit: Krista Kuniyoshi

ISBN: 978-1-5127-8206-6 (sc)
ISBN: 978-1-5127-8207-3 (hc)
ISBN: 978-1-5127-8205-9 (e)

Library of Congress Control Number: 2017904812

Print information available on the last page.

WestBow Press rev. date: 4/3/2017

Contents

Acknowledgments vii

Foreword ix

Introduction: Intentionality for Christ in the Four Seasons of
Spiritual Formation xiii

Chapter 1   Coming to Grips with Gospel Intentionality at
Midlife 1

Chapter 2   The Warlords of Waste in the Battle for the
Affections 18

Chapter 3   Gospel Transformation at Midlife: Repentance,
Healing, and Faith 42

Chapter 4   The Convergence of Experience and Grace 55

Chapter 5   This One Thing I Do 64

Conclusion: What is the Next Season of Spiritual Formation? 70

Bibliography 73

Appendix: Seasons One and Two Templates 78

Acknowledgments

My deep thanks to Christ Church staff and members involved in the last twenty years of spiritual formation classes for sharing your precious sense of intentionality for Christ from the heart. I have so much gratitude for my wife, Karen, who has helped me take aim in my calling as a husband, father, and grandfather, especially as a partner in the pastorate.

I am particularly grateful for my elders for "tithing" me five Sundays to invest in seminary teaching overseas since 2008. Dave and Cathy Bowman have helped me with intentionality in ministry by example and with counsel over the years. Finally, this and many projects could not be possible without the constant encouragement from Gary and Farole Haluska.

Foreword

The concern of the series on spiritual formation lies at the heart of the gospel. The gospel invites humans to draw near to God's revelation in Jesus Christ. This revelation is the revelation of the Triune God—Father, Son, and Holy Spirit. He who was, is, is to come, and ever will be invites human beings to connect with him, to see his glory and reflect it, and to partner with him as members of the body of the Lord Jesus Christ. The Church Father, Irenaeus (ca. 175), wrote, "For the glory of God is a living man; and the life of man consists in beholding God." (*AH* IV.20.7) The gospel truly opens human beings to a vision of God in Jesus Christ. It transforms a person's orientation from religion, which is man-centered, to revelation, which is God-centered.

Dr. Smart develops the process of this gradual reorientation as "Four Seasons" of the Christian life: Identity *in* Christ, Calling *to* Christ, Intentionality *for* Christ, and Legacy *from* Christ. The danger lurks continuously for Christian men and women to enjoy the spiritual benefits of the gospel without a true transformation. We often and easily deceive ourselves into acting and speaking as followers of Jesus Christ, while clinging to our old identity in Adam. The apostle Paul spoke of an inner battle that often leads to the negative observation: "What a wretched man I am! Who will rescue me from this body of death?" (Romans 7:24) The lessons on spiritual formation open a greater awareness of an inner struggle that grows in intensity as we become more mature in the faith. It is not until we see the fullness of Jesus Christ that we grow in intentionality and maturity, as John R. W. Stott observes:

> It is when people see Christ in his fullness that their faith, obedience and worship are stimulated and so they become mature. It is the Word of God, confirmed and enforced by the Spirit of God, which effectively matures and sanctifies the people of God. [1]

During the many years of midlife we see more clearly our identity in Christ and find our calling to Christ. In the intervening years, we learn to decenter our lives and passions. A new intentionality is borne. It is a time of internalization and evaluation, because so much of life turns out to be empty in comparison with the fullness that Christ offers. We find renewal by intensely looking at the things "above" of which Paul writes, "Since, then, you have been raised with Christ, set your hearts on things above, where Christ is seated at the right hand of God. Set your minds on things above, not on earthly things" (Colossians 3:1-2). We experience the glorious transformation and purification by the inner renewal of our soiled lives."Do not lie to each other, since you have taken off your old self with its practices and have put on the new self, which is being renewed in knowledge in the image of its Creator" (Colossians 3:9). We also find Scripture becomes more precious as we spend more time reflecting on the Word of God, "Let the word of Christ dwell in you richly as you teach and admonish one another with all wisdom,

---

[1] "The Langham Trust Strategic Vision," http://us.langham.org/who-we-are/vision-mission-2/

and as you sing psalms, hymns and spiritual songs with gratitude in your hearts to God" (Colossians 3:16).

The German pastor-scholar Dietrich Bonhoeffer, who lost his life by resisting the Nazi regime in 1945, observed so well on Christian intentionality. Eric Metaxas recounts in a recent biography on Bonhoeffer,

> [Bonhoeffer] dismissed the standard responses to what they were up against and showed why each would fail. "Who stands fast?" he asked. "Only the man whose final standard is not his reason, his principles, his conscience, his freedom, or his virtue, but who is ready to sacrifice all this when he is called to obedient and responsible action in faith and in exclusive allegiance to God—the responsible man, who tries to make his whole life an answer to the question and call of God."[2]

I close on a personal note. Over the last ten years my wife, Evona, and I have come to know Pastor Bob and have appreciated his ministry in and the fellowship of the Christ Church community in Normal, Illinois. I have witnessed his passion for spiritual transformation. It is grounded in the Word and flourishes in individuals and in the community. I thank the Lord for his fruitful ministry.

—Willem A. VanGemeren, PhD, professor emeritus of Old Testament, Trinity Evangelical Divinity School, Deerfield, Illinois

---

[2] Eric Metaxas, *Bonhoeffer: Pastor, Mentor. Prophet, Spy* (Nashville: Thomas Nelson, 2010), 446.

Introduction

Intentionality for Christ in the Four Seasons of Spiritual Formation

Season Three of Spiritual Formation

In my first book in this series of four on the Christian's spiritual formation *Embracing Your Identity in Christ: Renouncing Lies and Foolish Strategies*, I wrote:

> Our identity, besides being one of the most precious things to prevent from theft, crisis, or loss, is extremely important to God. The Father has given His each of His children a personal identity in Christ that will shape them on their journey to heaven. If in the process of identity formation we ignore what God says concerning our identity, then we may expect confusion in the other three seasons of spiritual formation from adolescence to old age. (See chart below for Identity in Christ, Calling to Christ, Intentionality for Christ, and Legacy from Christ.)

4 SEASONS OF SPIRITUAL FORMATION

IDENTITY *in* CHRIST
Who am I?

- Names
- Family
- God's Image
- Glorious Ruins
- Renounce Lie
- Justified
- Adopted
- Sanctified

CALLING *to* CHRIST
Where's my place?

- God's Summons
- Central/Peripheral
- Kairotic Events
- 3 Longings
- Micah 6:8
- Prophet/Priest/King
- Apostolic Band
- Agora (Streets)

INTENTIONALITY *for* CHRIST
What's my best aim?

- Gifted & Experienced
- Regrets
- Busyness
- Fear
- Resignation
- Faith/Hope/Love
- Mid-Life Bucket Lists
- Greatest Contribution

LEGACY *from* CHRIST
What's my message?

- My Treasury
- Succession
- Influence
- Will for Others
- The Jordan River
- Benediction
- Deliver Mail
- Letting Go

Just after birth or adoption, a child is given her first sense of identity from her parents. Identity formation, however, is a much longer process. When Jesus Christ was approximately thirty years of age, the Father spoke of His identity at His baptism just before Jesus entered fully into His primary calling. In the same way, a clear sense of our identity in Christ ought to precede our calling formation to Christ. It is during this foundational season of identity formation that Satan challenges each of us, as he did our Lord. The devil's first attacks were aimed at Jesus's identity when two times he cast doubt about who He was: "*If* you are the Son of God ..." (Luke 4:3, 9).[3]

The evil trinity—the world, the flesh, and the devil—is seeking to destroy us in each season of our spiritual formation. In the spring they mess with our *identity*, in the summer our *calling*, in the autumn with our *intentionality*, and in the winter with our preparation for heaven— our *legacy*. The world ushers Christians in this age bracket near to yet another pit, the flesh persuades us to fall in, and the devil pushes us over the edge. "The pit," as it were, represents an aimless waste collection of unused gifts, time, and resources that could have been invested more strategically for Christ's honor and the gospel's advance.

This third season of spiritual formation for the Christian, Intentionality for Christ, is the third of four seasons of gospel transformation meant to shape us into the glorious likeness of Jesus Christ. This season largely takes place between thirty-five and sixty-five years of age. It assumes we have a reasonable grip on our identity in Christ and our calling to Christ, but renewal is needed on these. Intentionality for Christ is a season of spiritual formation that will wonderfully prepare us for the last major season of spiritual formation; namely, legacy from Christ.

This book is designed for a leader or individual to begin each chapter with prayer, and to ask the discussion questions provided at the end of each chapter in order to help each person discover and write out a sense of one's intentionality for Christ in this midlife season of spiritual formation. The goal is that by the end, each

---

[3] Scripture quotations are from the ESV Bible (The Holy Bible, English Standard Version). Crossway: 2001.

person can use the template provided in the last chapter to write out their spiritual intentions for Christ.

In order to improve upon our effort, chapter 1 explains how to come to grips with gospel intentionality at midlife. Chapter 2 addresses the warlords of waste in the battle for the affections. Chapter 3 offers gospel transformation in midlife through repentance, healing, and faith. Chapter 4 examines the convergence of experience and faith by understanding our life stories. Finally, in chapter 5 we will whittle away at unnecessary extras by aiming at one task—namely, to cultivate gospel transformation.

In all this, we are seeking God's grace—the power of His Spirit, the agency of His Word, the mystery of His providence, and the caring concern of His people—to transform each of us more permanently, uniquely, and heartily to invest God's resources, gifts, and time for Christ in the best way.

Wisdom teaches a Christian to begin by asking God who he or she is and where his or her place is before asking the next two major questions of the Christian life: How do I steward all my gifts, resources, and efforts well in the light of eternity (intentionality)? And what inheritance, testament, and benediction do I leave behind as I prepare to cross the river of death and into heaven's gates (legacy)?

Embracing your godly intentions for Christ in this season of your life has much more weight than you may give it at this time. It is transforms us in midlife, culminates well into our sixties, and it progressively enriches us with an abundant life well into our legacy from Christ (the fourth season of spiritual formation). How awesome our end on earth will be when we live intentionally for Christ in this long, third season of spiritual formation! When we will come before at the end, we want to hear Christ say to each of us, "Well done, good and faithful servant" (Matthew 25:21). So let's begin with asking what are our intentions for Christ, and how shall we take aim?

Let's begin by coming to grips with the gospel, and intentionality for Christ, at midlife.

Chapter 1

Coming to Grips with Gospel Intentionality at Midlife

When I was in my mid-thirties, I was facing up to reality. I had preached at my parents' funerals one year apart, my wife was pregnant with twins and often sick, our new puppy barked too much, and ministry was harder than I had imagined. I needed help in coming to grips with the beginnings of midlife and what I was living for.

In every transitional point in my life, when I have moved from one season of spiritual formation to the next, Dave and Cathy Bowman have been there for me. When I came to Christ, they shaped my identity in Christ. Dave taught me to discover and renounce my core lie. When I followed God's call on my life to enter full-time vocational ministry, Dave had me saturate myself in the Bible's teaching on calling and write out my sense of personal calling. At this point, I was a pastor of a small church with a family of five children. I was struggling to come to grips with my story and my shattered dream of what my life was supposed to look like. I'll never forget Dave's tender strength when he pointed his finger, referring to my interpretation of my childhood and my dream for life, and his sure voice said, "That's not reality."

This chapter introduces the reader to the challenges that occur in midlife, which the Christian must come to grips with. It begins with a brief definition of gospel intentionality, asks the central question in this season of spiritual formation, addresses the challenges we face at midlife, calls for the need to engage in spiritual warfare, and invites the readers to take aim.

What Is Gospel Intentionality?

Gospel intentionality is a season of spiritual formation at midlife, from around age thirty-five to sixty-five years. It is a season of life when the gospel transforms us from one degree of glory to the next as we focus on Christ (2 Corinthians 3:17–18). Whereas the first season of identity in Christ is about being and position, the second season of spiritual formation is about doing and performance. In this season, we settle into the place God puts us. Each of these seasons is an experience of gospel transformation. The third season, then, of intentionality, is about narrowing down what we do for Christ. It is about taking aim in the transformation process.

Intentionality, besides being a philosophical concept, is defined as a disposition of the will; as a noun, it is the state of being volitional in nature. The Christian has new affections for Christ and a disposition to will the best and most excellent, God-glorifying, and God-satisfying life possible. The Latin etymology of intentionality indicates the relevant idea of directedness or tension arising from aiming toward a particular target. There is always a tension in the Christian's experience. He or she is already God's pleasure but seeks to please Him in areas not yet pleasing to Christ in his or her will. A Christian who is well grounded in his or her identity in Christ and solidified in his or her calling to Christ will be intentional for Christ as the last season of spiritual formation draws near. This definition, then, explains how a Christian with a disposition to live intentionally for Christ will ask a simple and vital question.

Intentionality's Question

The key question at midlife is this: What does it mean to steward and aim all my resources, gifts, and efforts with gospel intentionality in light of old age and eternity beyond? What am I aiming for?

Intentionality is about aim, which means it is a question of ethics. In Christian ethics, the controlling purpose is the glory of Christ, the impelling motive is the love of Christ, and the directing principle is the will of Christ. God is the *summun bonum* or highest good. John Calvin reasoned like this:

> If God contains the fullness of all good things in Himself like an inexhaustible fountain, nothing beyond Him is to be sought by those who strive after the highest good and all the elements of happiness.[4]

Our middle years represent the longest season of our life when we most likely will not change locations or vocations very much. It is in this season that many lose aim because they look back on our lives in a wrong way, looking for happiness in all the wrong places. We are tempted to look back after putting our hands to the plow. When God called Lot out of Sodom and Gomorrah, he was told to make sure none of his family looked back, lest they be turned into pillars of salt. Unfortunately, "Lot's wife, behind him, looked back, and she became a pillar of salt" (Genesis 19:26). She couldn't move ahead into the future for her Lord.

At midlife, we are tempted to quit the Christian race, but we must remain on the course set before us to press on to better days. Midlife is the age of ambivalence. We have already arrived, but not yet. In fact, the time between Christ's first and second comings, which

---

[4] Calvin, John. *Institutes of the Christian Religion*. Vol. 2. Ed. John T. McNeill, trans. Ford Lewis Battles. Philadelphia, PA: Westminster Press, 1960, 1,005.

we now live, is called the age of the "already, not yet." The "already but not yet" paradigm was first developed by Princeton theologian Gerhardus Vos early in the twentieth century. In the 1950s, George Eldon Ladd popularized the concept when he described the kingdom in scripture both as a realm presently entered and as one entered in the future. Ladd concluded that the kingdom of God is both present and future—already, but not yet.[5]

Paul grieved over a coworker who deserted him at midlife for the love of the world. Some middle-aged folks are drawn away by a love for the world from the initial calling to Christ they followed in their twenties or thirties. The ways and comforts of the world are too tempting for some people. Paul wrote to Timothy about the sad news. "For Demas, in love with this present world, has deserted me and [is] gone" (2 Timothy 4:10).

When Eric Liddell, "the flying Scot," was asked the secret to winning a gold medal in the four-hundred-meter race in the Olympics race, he said the first two hundred meters he ran as fast as he possibly could. The second two hundred meters, he said, "by God's grace I ran even faster." Many Christians are happy to quote Liddell's most famous lines from *Chariots of Fire*. "God made me fast. And when I run, I feel his pleasure."

You and I may have run a fast, hard race until this point, and we have sensed God's pleasure in making us fast. There have been many accomplishments and fruitful endeavors thus far that make us "raise our Ebenezer." We sing the beautiful verse from the hymn "Come Thou Fount," which was composed by the Second Great Awakening preacher Asahel Nettleton. "Here I raise my Ebenezer; Hither by Thine help I'm come." Ebenezer was the name of a stone. The name is from the event when Samuel took a stone and set it up between Mizpah and Shen and called its name *Ebenezer*; for he said,

---

[5] Ladd, George Eldon. *The Gospel of the Kingdom: Scriptural Studies in the Kingdom of God*. Grand Rapids, MI: Wm. B. Eerdmans Publishing, 1959, 41.

"Till now the LORD has helped us" (1 Samuel 7:12).[6] So we raise our Ebenezer at midlife, but we still have the second half of life to run. There is a prize that awaits us from Christ.

When Liddell left for China as a missionary, he bid farewell at an Edinburgh train station under the shadow of the castle there. He leaned out the opened window of the train to lead a large crowd in singing "Jesus Shall Reign." The next stop was China, followed by the Shantung Compound and suffering as a martyr, and his final stop was heaven.[7] He won another medal in the presence of Christ because he was running in such a way for another prize.[8]

How will you run the second half of your race? Let us say, like Liddell, "by God's grace I run even faster." Jesus began to witness this brokenness in people to quit halfway among many of His followers, so He challenged them to not be distracted as He took aim for His final and greatest work. He called for intentionality from His disciples.

As the time drew near for his return to heaven, he moved steadily onward toward Jerusalem with an iron will ... But Jesus told him, "Anyone who lets himself be distracted from the work I plan for him is not fit for the Kingdom of God." (Luke 9:51, 62)

---

[6] The eighteenth-century pastor and author Robert Robinson, who penned the words at age twenty-two in the year 1757, wrote the hymn "Come Thou Fount," which was composed by Asahel Nettleton in the 1840s.
[7] http://www.albertmohler.com/2016/08/12/god-made-china-eric-liddell-beyond-olympic-glory/.
[8] 1 Corinthians 9:24.

Coming to Grips with Midlife's Commonalities

What are some of the common challenges that Christians in midlife experience that make their former intentions for Christ less attractive? Having led this spiritual formation group for many years in the past, I can recall most of the challenges people mentioned.

Midlife, for most of us, is a season of routine and endurance when retirement and ease seem more and more attractive. We will experience a noticeable decline in health and at least a slight increase in weight. By forty-five, the body's metabolism slows down, causing weight gain. It is a great time to take aim and to get serious about diet and exercise. Our middle years are our best decades to make our greatest contributions in our callings, but it is a season marked by loss. There is a common loss of health, hope, parents on earth, children at home, friendships nearby, and more. Although this will vary according to the individual, these losses are a common part of life. Only an intentional approach to overcome these challenges will make this season transformational for the subsequent spiritual formation season of legacy.

We are vulnerable without an intentional and offensive approach to these challenges in middle years. Fleeing in fear and shifting the blame in anger are both approaches that get us nowhere. Ella Wheeler Wilcox's poem communicates that ultimately it our intentionality that determines the direction we will go, and alignment with the will of God is a refusal to be tossed to and fro by every wind that threatens to blow us off course. She wrote:

> One ship drives east and another drives west
> With the self-same winds that blow;
> 'Tis the set of the sails
> And not the gales
> That tells them the way to go.

Like the winds of the sea are the winds of fate
As we voyage along through life;
'Tis the set of the soul
That decides its goal
And not the calm or the strife.[9]

What is the set of your sails, the set of your soul? Whatever rules or governs your course is your god, but let us not allow anything to rule us—not betrayal, not loss, not empty-nest syndrome, not death of parent(s), not care-taking fatigue, not shattered dreams, nor regrets. For with gospel intentionality our souls can still be set with intentionality for Christ.

Spiritual Warfare

The evil trinity—the world, the flesh, and the devil—seeks to destroy us in this season, and we must fight. We must be strong in the strength of God's might, and not try to overcome independent of Him. We must choose the weapons of our warfare and not merely search the Internet for simple advice. There are thoughts to be taken captive (2 Corinthians 10:4–5), promises in God's word to be trusted, and prayers to be answered. In other words, intentional living is not only beneficial; it is also necessary because we are in a battle. You must be committed to battle against "the warlords of waste," which we shall address in the next chapter.

---

[9] Ella Wheeler Wilcox, "The Winds of Fate" in *World Voices* (New York, NY: Hearst's International Library Company, 1916)

Taking Aim

The battle we are in during midlife is about aim. If we do not aim well, then we are no threat to the kingdom of darkness. If we take aim, then the joy of the Holy Spirit will increase within us. Our faces will be radiant when we are looking to Christ (Psalm 34:5), and the joy of and in the Lord will be our strength (Nehemiah 8:10).

According to Alexander Whyte:

> Persecution from England and controversy at home so embittered Rutherford's sweet and gracious spirit ... few and far between. But let him away out into pure theology, and, especially, let him get his wings on the person, and the work, and the glory of Christ, and few theologians of any age or any school rise to a larger air, or command a wider scope, or discover a clearer eye of speculation than Rutherford, till we feel exactly like the laird of Glanderston, who, when Rutherford left a controversial passage in a sermon and went on to speak of Christ, cried out in the church—"Ay, hold you there, minister; you are all right there!"[10]

Hold your gaze on Christ. Take aim.

Anyone in this world without aim has no place or purpose to give life meaning under God. The Beatles describe the fallen condition of an aimless life in their catchy song, "Nowhere Man:"

> He's a real nowhere man
> Sitting in his nowhere land

---

[10] Alexander Whyte, *Samuel Rutherford* (London: Oliphant Anderson and Ferrier, 1894), p. 12.

Making all his nowhere plans
For nobody
Doesn't have a point of view
Knows not where he's going to
Isn't he a bit like you and me?[11]

God has rescued us from a life without purpose or place. God ordains every day for His purposes to be fulfilled in the place He puts us. Everything matters, and is shot through with meaning and opportune moments that count for eternity. This is why the Psalmist in his latter years estimates the average person's longevity and prays: "Teach us to number our days that we may get a heart of wisdom" (Psalm 90:12). The Psalmist, probably Moses, asks that God's work be shown to His people and their children. He desires that the favor of the Lord our God be upon us, and that God will establish the work of our hands (Psalm 90:16–17).

The Christian is no longer a "nowhere man," who "knows not where he's going to." God has called the Christian to a place with a purpose. The Christian is a steward with treasure to invest until he or she reports to show the Master what was gained (Matthew 25:20–23). The Christian ought not to wait around aimlessly for retirement years that check out of living intentionally for Christ. John Piper exhorts the Christian against such a wasteful approach to spiritual formation. He writes:

> I will tell you what a tragedy is. I will show you how to waste your life. Consider a story from the February 1998 edition of *Reader's Digest*, which tells about a couple who took early retirement from their jobs in the Northeast five years ago when he was

---

[11] John Lennon and Paul McCartney, "Nowhere Man" in *Rubber Soul* album (Abbey Road Studios: EMI Records, October 12, 1965).

59 and she was 51. Now they live in Punta Gorda, Florida, where they cruise on their 30 foot trawler, play softball and collect shells. At first, when I read it I thought it might be a joke. A spoof on the American Dream. But it wasn't. Tragically, this was the dream: Come to the end of your life—your one and only precious, God-given life-and let the last great work of your life, before you give an account to your Creator, be this: playing softball and collecting shells. Picture them before Christ at the great day of judgment: "Look, Lord. See my shells." That is a tragedy. And people today are spending billions of dollars to persuade you to embrace that tragic dream. Over against that, I put my protest: Don't buy it. Don't waste your life.[12]

The wisdom literature of the Bible instructs us on how to overcome in the various seasons of life by taking aim. In Psalm 71, for example, the Psalmist prays,

O God, from my youth you have taught me, and I still proclaim your wondrous deeds. So even in old age and gray hairs, O God, do not forsake me, until I proclaim your might to another generation, your power to all those to come. (Psalm 71:17–18)

In Psalm 78:1, as well, the Psalmist asks others in midlife to, "Give ear, O my people, to my teaching; incline your ears to the words of my mouth!" He takes a willful aim when he says, "We will not hide them from our children, but tell the next generation the

---

[12] John Piper, *Don't Waste Your Life* (Wheaton, IL: Crossway Books, 2007), pp. 45–46.

glorious deeds of the Lord and His might, and the wonders He has done" (Psalm 78:4).

Each morning, in solitude with God, I take aim. Gospel saturation fuels me to make plans born out of prayer. As I pray for my five children, their spouses, and my twelve grandchildren, I consider the needs of each person. I make an intentional plan, then, how I might invest in their lives. It might be to ask them out on a date, or it may be gift for them. As I pray for my wife, I ask for specific requests for her and consider something we could do together for our marriage. If husbands are not intentional, they become as silent as Adam in the presence of the serpent and suffer the consequences of a wife crouched to control them.

The fictitious and humorous story is told of Judgment Day. Everybody on earth dies and goes to heaven. God comes and says, "I want the men to make two lines; one line for the men that led their women without being dominated on earth, and the other line for the men that were controlled by their women. Also, I want all the women to go with Saint Peter." There was a lot of shuffling about in heaven until all was settled. The women were gone, and there were two lines. The line of men who were controlled by their wives was one hundred miles long, but the line of men lovingly leading their wives consisted of only one man.

God was not surprised to see the length of the one line, but he inquired of the man in the small one. "Tell them, my son, how did you manage to be the only one in that line?" The man said, "I don't know. My wife told me to stand here." If husbands are not motivated by the gospel to love and plan intentional ways to edify their wives and children, then they will suffer the consequences of frenetic women unable to go off duty. Such husbands may say they are the head of the home, but their wives are the necks. They turn the head wherever they wish.

Christians in midlife must arise and take aim because they have years of experience in their callings. They have become experts in their fields. They are paid more because their knowledge and skills are at their zenith and prime. Charlie Steinmetz was a dwarf and terribly deformed, but what he lacked physically he made up for mentally. Few people knew more about electricity than Mr. Steinmetz. Henry Ford realized this and hired him to build those vast generators that would run their first plant in Dearborn, Michigan. Along came Steinmetz, who, with remarkable genius, put together those vast, wonderful pieces of machinery that make great profit for the Ford Motor Company.

One day, suddenly, without announcement, the place ground to a stop. Ford hired a few ordinary mechanics and a number of hard-working helpers, but no one seemed to be able to find the problem. He finally pressed his friendship with Mr. Steinmetz and asked him to come and do a little repair work. Steinmetz fiddled around with this gauge, tinkered with that motor, tried this button, did a little wiring, tinkered with this switch, and threw the master switch. In a matter of a few hours everything was fixed and the motors were running again.

Within a few days, Steinmetz mailed Ford a bill for $10,000. Although Henry Ford was eminently wealthy, he balked at paying such an exorbitant amount of money for what appeared to be a little bit of work. And so he wrote a letter to his friend and he included the bill. "Charlie: It seems awfully steep, this $10,000, for a man who for just a little while tinkered around with a few motors." Steinmetz wrote a new bill and sent it back to Mr. Ford, "Henry: For tinkering around with motors, $10; for knowing where to tinker, $9,990.00."[13]

About once a month I sit with an Old Testament scholar, Dr. Willem VanGemeren of TEDS (Trinity Evangelical Divinity School), to talk about everything under the sun. He is my Qoheleth from the book of Ecclesiastes. He is an expert in his field. When I arrive from the long drive out to his home in the country, he gives

---

[13] Swindoll, Charles (1998-11-20). The Tale of the Tardy Oxcart (Swindoll Leadership Library) (pp. 321–322). Thomas Nelson. Kindle Edition.

me a warm Dutch greeting as if I were his son. Immediately we are driving his golf cart around his land, and he names every kind of vegetation and tree he has planted and arranged beautifully. Of course, that leads into a conversation about God's glory in creation and his intentionality to glorify God in all of life. We usually, then, sit in his gazebo or porch, he with a cat on his lap, to talk about the latest scholarly books he is writing and reading from biblical theology to contemporary cultural analysis. Evona, his dear wife, brings us coffee and treats.

Willem is evidence that the Christian life is anything but boredom. He is in his middle seventies, but he works like a man should in his forties. Willem has spiritual children who were trained, awarded doctorates, and serve all over the world. He shares about his global efforts in teaching seminary courses as a missionary and those ethnic issues. We discuss spiritual matters in our lives and in the local church we both attend. Willem amazes me with his fortitude and intentionality in his seventies to advance God's kingdom. I want to follow his example and learn everything possible. He is my Qoheleth for this season of intentionality. He teaches me that the Christian life is an adventure.

Spiritual formation is a process that awakens the Christian's longings to live for eternal consequences, to see death as gain, and to rise above the apathetic living of our culture. We do not have to surrender to the postmodern malaise of apathy. Henri Nouwen described the primary condition of our postmodern culture, as he saw it, as one of apathy and boredom. This condition is largely a result of the "broken bow" of intentionality. Nouwen wrote:

> Why should a man marry and have children, study and build a career; why should he invent new techniques, build new institutions, and develop new ideas—when he doubts if there will be a tomorrow which can guarantee the value of human effort?

Crucial here for nuclear man is the lack of a sense of continuity, which is so vital for a creative life. He finds himself part of a nonhistory in which only the sharp moment of the here and now is valuable. For nuclear man life easily becomes a bow whose string is broken and from which no arrow can fly. In his dislocated state he becomes paralyzed. His reactions are not anxiety and joy, which were so much a part of existential man, but apathy and boredom.[14]

The Christian life begins at the cross where Christ rescues us from a wasted and apathetic life. Christ calls us to joy through meaningful suffering; to living for the joy set before us when we see Christ face to Face. Oddly enough, the cross is the beginning of joyful living, and our sinful nature must die there. In the words of Dietrich Bonhoeffer,

> *The cross is not the terrible end to an otherwise God-fearing and happy life, but it meets us at the beginning of our communion with Christ. When Christ calls a man, he bids him come and die.*[15]

The apostle Paul expressed and testified about the joyful living that began at the cross. The present value of the cross gave him an intentional way of living. It motivated him to run even faster at midlife and brought him to a satisfying finish. In his first letter he testified:

> I have been crucified with Christ. It is no longer I who live, but Christ who lives in me. And the life I now live in the flesh I live by faith in the Son of God,

---

[14] Henri J. M. Nouwen, *The Wounded Healer: Ministry in Contemporary Society* (New York, NY: Doubleday, 1972, repr. 1990), pp. 8–9.

[15] Dietrich Bonhoeffer, *The Cost of Discipleship* (New York, NY: Macmillan, 1963, repr. 1979), p. 99.

who loved me and gave himself for me. (Galatians 2:19–20)

He had a whole new relation to the world. He said: "Far be it from me to boast except in the cross of our Lord Jesus Christ, by which the world has been crucified to me, and I to the world" (Galatians 6:14).

In the middle of his Christian life, the season of intentionality, he wrote:

> I do not account my life of any value nor as precious to myself, if only I may finish my course and the ministry that I received from the Lord Jesus, to testify to the gospel of the grace of God. (Acts 20:24)

So, that by the end of his life, he could write his final letter and say:

> I have fought the good fight, I have finished the race, I have kept the faith. Henceforth there is laid up for me the crown of righteousness, which the Lord, the righteous judge, will award to me on that Day. (2 Timothy 4:7–8)

Dr. Howard Hendricks shares how he lost one of his best friends, a woman eighty-six years old. Hendricks that she was "the most exciting lay teacher I've ever been exposed to." May her tribe increase! He remembered her this way:

> The last time I saw her on planet Earth was at one of those aseptic Christian parties. We were sitting there on eggshells, looking pious, when she walked in and said, "Well, Hendricks, I haven't seen you for

a long time. What are the five best books you've read in the past year?"

She had a way of changing a group's dynamics. Her philosophy was, Let's not bore each other with each other; let's get into a discussion, and if we can't find anything to discuss, let's get into an argument.

> She was eighty-three on her last trip to the Holy Land. She went there with a group of NFL football players. One of my most vivid memories of her is seeing her out front yelling back to them, "Come on, men, get with it!"

> She died in her sleep at her daughter's home in Dallas. Her daughter told me that just before she died, she had written out her goals for the next ten years.[16]

This chapter introduced the reader to the challenges that occur in midlife, which the Christian must come to grips with. It began with a brief definition of gospel intentionality, asked the central question in this season of spiritual formation, addressed the challenges we face at midlife, called for the need to engage in spiritual warfare, and invited the readers to take aim.

What's your aim? The winds of culture and circumstances blow where they will, but how will you "set your sails" in midlife? Becoming intentional about the gospel is a matter of living for "Christ, who is your life." When He appears, you will appear with Him in glory (Colossians 3:4). Since the Christian life is by nature a spiritual

---

[16] Howard Hendricks, *Teaching to Change Lives: Seven Proven Ways to Make Your Teaching Come Alive* (Sisters, OR: Multnomah Publishers, 1987), p. 23.

battle, in the next chapter we consider how to slay the "warlords of waste." In order to clarify our aim and sense a convergence of all God's graces coming together with intentionality (chapter 4), we must repent of ways we justify ourselves, hide our glory, and deaden our longings (chapter 3). Only then will we recover our sense of need for the gospel to transform our hearts in the final chapters.

Discussion Group Questions:

1. How has your identity in Christ and your calling to Christ helped prepare you for this third season of spiritual formation?
2. What is your understanding of gospel intentionality?
3. What is your aim in life now as you consider all the experiences and resources that God has given you at this point in your Christian life?
4. What are some of the challenges you are facing in midlife?
5. How is God calling you to engage more fully in spiritual warfare?
6. Are you willing to run, by God's grace, the second half of your race even faster?
7. Would you consider practicing the spiritual discipline of solitude?

Suggested Practice for Solitude with God:

Begin with silence in God's presence. Listen for questions that may arise in your heart to ask the Lord about. Meditate on scripture. Finally, engage in prayers of adoration, receiving and giving forgiveness, thanksgiving, and petitions or requests.

Chapter 2

The Warlords of Waste in the Battle for the Affections

Warlords and Affections

The Bible begins with two thin pages of shalom in Eden, and ends with two thin pages of heaven. Everything in between is a war for our affections. If we are to overcome, then we must fight. In the words of C. T. Studd:

> Let us not slide through this world and then slip quietly into heaven without having blown the trumpet loud and long for our Redeemer, Jesus Christ. Let us see to it that the devil will hold a thanksgiving service in hell when he gets news of our departure from the field of battle.[17]

Warlords are leaders of military groups who are not officially recognized and who fight against leaders, groups, and governments. Warlords are aggressive regional commanders, who attack the established order and often suppress people in their areas of influence.

---

[17] Quoted on *GoodReads website*: https://www.goodreads.com/quotes/641387-let-us-not-glide-through-this-world-and-then-slip

Bosnia, Serbia, and several similar countries used to be ruled by warlord factions in the 1990s until NATO and expeditionary forces brought about factional demise.

Warlords, then, in the spiritual context for this chapter, refer to powerful and sinful influences that attack the Christian's holy affections for Christ in midlife. These "warlords of waste," as I call them, open us to the lordship of domineering demons that seek to oppress our lives by keeping our affections off Christ and on to lesser things. They are sinful tendencies in midlife that give the devil a foothold in our lives in order to waste our precious contributions to the kingdom of God in the most productive season of gospel living.

Jonathan Edwards believed, as I do, that true Christianity chiefly consists in our affections because our affections largely determine our wills.[18] The initial affections we received when we were born again by the Holy Spirit are called in the Bible, "the fruit of the Spirit." God gave us holy affections of love, joy, peace, and so forth. (Galatians 5:22–24) These precious affections are a dreadful threat to our sinful nature and to Satan. Our sinful nature wars against our new nature in an irreconcilable war. We must put them to death, put them away (Colossians 3:5, 8). If Satan can kill them, he has destroyed your will for Christ. Matthew Henry commented on the necessity of putting our sinful nature and tendencies to death. He wrote:

> Mortify them, kill them, suppress them, as weeds or vermin, which spread and destroy all about them. Continual opposition must be made to all corrupt workings, and no provision made for carnal indulgences. Occasions of sin must be avoided: the

---

[18] Jonathan Edwards, *Religious Affections* (New Haven, MA: Yale University Press, 1959). John E. Smith, editor, *The Works of Jonathan Edwards*, Volume Two, p. 95.

lusts of the flesh, and the love of the world; and covetousness, which is idolatry; love of present good, and of outward enjoyments. It is necessary to mortify sins, because if we do not kill them, they will kill us.[19]

Therefore, the oppression of our new nature or holy affections for Christ is the aim of the warlords of waste. If evil can kill spiritual affections in the heart of the Christian in this season of spiritual formation, our intentionality for Christ is sorely diminished and weakened. In midlife, Christians often grow weak in holy affections for this very reason; namely, we give up the fight. In the words of C. S. Lewis, "The long, dull, monotonous years of middle-aged prosperity or middle-aged adversity are excellent campaigning weather for the devil."[20]

We, therefore, are going to consider four mighty warlords of waste because they are the most common enemies that war against your affections for Christ in this season of spiritual formation. These mighty warlords are control, regret, fear, and busyness.

The Mighty Warlords of Midlife

We will ask how so many live without intentionality for Christ in midlife, yet end in retirement seemingly living for self. The following pages seek to free the anxiety, anger, and bitterness of powerlessness that is rooted in our attempt to *control* everything. These warlords have many citizens of the kingdom squished between two thieves— *regret* from the past and *fear* of the future—while stuck in the milieu

---

[19] Matthew Henry, *Matthew Henry's Commentary* (Col 3:5-8)
[20] C.S. Lewis, *The Screwtape Letters* "Letter XXVIII."

of *busyness* of the present. These four warlords of waste will make your spiritual life miserable.

The Warlord of Control

The first warlord of waste that battles our affections for Christ is control. If you seek control, your greatest nightmare is uncertainty. People around you feel condemned, and your companion will be worry. Our efforts to give us a sense of being in control because we believe we keep everything intact, but there is no freedom in this. What do we fear the loss of losing most? What, if we lost it, would make life not worth living? We must lose it for Jesus's sake in order to keep it. A sense of control functions to provide us with a sense of confidence and safety, but this is something only Jesus can provide.

> Whatever controls us is our lord. The person who seeks power is controlled by power. The person who seeks acceptance is controlled by the people he or she wants to please. We do not control ourselves. We are controlled by the lord of our lives.[21]

The curse on femininity is that a woman be crouched to control her primary relationships in life (Genesis 3:16), which pushes people away from the very relationship and intimacy a woman longs for. Controlling men have been also caused grief and been called micromanagers, hotheads, and threatening taskmasters.

It is evident when a controlling spirit is oppressing us. Three evidences of a person's deep commitment to control others and circumstances are anxiety, anger, and bitterness. When our goals

---

[21] Rebecca Pippert, *Out of the Saltshaker* (Downers Grove, IL: InterVarsity Press, 1979), p. 53.

are blocked, we will certainly experience an initial anxiety. Anxiety gives birth to anger, and prolonged anger to bitterness. The "roots of bitterness" spring up and cause trouble, and by it many are defiled. We are to see to it that no one fails to obtain the grace of God by removing such bitterness—roots and all. The writer of the letter to the Hebrews said: "See to it that no one fails to obtain the grace of God; that no 'root of bitterness' springs up and causes trouble, and by it many become defiled" (Hebrews 12:15).

Control functions for us to get what we want without trusting the Lord with our longings. Controlling others may have appeared to work for us in the past, and so we become skilled at manipulation by using sweetness, Christian language, or by threats of the law. One way or another, control is an illusion that we don't need to depend on God to give us what we long for and to make circumstances go our way.

Control is a warlord of waste because it robs our affections for Christ and deadens our longings by turning them into demands. How can we slay these in the battle for renewing our affections for Christ? The practice of these two disciplines, in particular, will help us in this regard; namely, embracing the sorrow of unmet longings in a godly manner and "disillusioning" ourselves from thinking we can control people and circumstances. These two practices will lead to godly intentionality and Spirit-filled freedom.

Embrace the Sorrow of Unmet Longings

When we are willing to admit we cannot control others and circumstances to get our way, we are admitting our powerlessness. Facing powerlessness is a step in the right direction, if we embrace the sorrow of unmet longings. Powerlessness without godly sorrow over the sin of trying to control can lead to three incorrect reactions. What are common ways people react to powerlessness? When we refuse to relinquish control, we tend to react in three unhealthy ways; namely, we dissociate, we act like a martyr, or we become belligerent.

One reaction to feeling powerless is to dissociate and sort of numb our longings. We simply go through the motions and avoid coming present to our situation. It is like driving a long stretch of highway and wondering afterwards where we have been. Some people just check out emotionally without any affection for Christ and lose a sense of direction and purpose in life.

A second response to powerlessness is to continue serving others in a way that does not let them help or comfort us, while trying to make them pay for our service. In this case, the person nurtures a self-righteousness that they deserve help and comfort, but is still demanding others to pay for it. An example is the wife or mother who dutifully makes dinner for the family, but her suffering in front of them makes them feel guilty for receiving the meal.

If dissociation or martyrdom isn't the strategy for coping, then belligerence can evolve over time. In the Old Testament Samson was made to feel his loss of power when his hair was cut off. He was chained up for a season until his strength and hair grew back. Seizing to make others pay for it, he pushed two pillars in a stadium until all the people inside were crushed to pieces.

All three of these reactions are refusals to surrender control. All control is in one way or another arrogance. It is presumptuous because only God is in sovereign control. James rebukes this illusion in those who assume they can make economic gains without acknowledging that it only if God is willing that we will go to a place and make some money. He wrote:

> Come now, you who say, 'Today or tomorrow we will go into such and such a town and spend a year there and trade and make a profit'—yet you do not know what tomorrow will bring. What is your

life? For you are a mist that appears for a little time
and then vanishes. Instead you ought to say, "If the
Lord wills, we will live and do this or that." (James
4:1–15)

We ought to get used to saying the old Latin phrase, *Deo Volente*—God willing, which is a way of saying, "If the Lord wills, we will live and do this or that." By embracing sorrow in a godly manner we are experiencing true repentance (2 Corinthians 7:11). If God is not willing to meet our longings yet, we must acknowledge we are not in control. We are also giving up our illusion of control, and acknowledging God is sovereign.

God reads the inward groans of our wordless longings with wisdom and love, causing all things to work together for our good. To embrace the sorrow of an unmet longing before God makes us realize that it is God we really desire. Those who mourn are blessed, like the Man of Sorrows. Herman Mellville in his book *Redburn* wrote: "And not til we know, that one grief outweighs ten thousand joys, will we become what Christianity is striving to make us."[22]

The Discipline of Disillusionment

We move from anxiety, anger, and bitterness by losing the control we never had in the first place. Besides admitting our powerlessness and embracing the sorrow of unmet longings, we can become free from control strategies through another discipline. In *My Utmost for His Highest*, Oswald Chambers asserts that Christ brings His disciples through a disillusioning process. Chambers called it the discipline of disillusionment. He wrote:

---

[22] Herman Mellville, *Redburn*, (Chicago, IL: Northwestern University Press, 1969, repr. 1993), p. 293.

Disillusionment means that there are no more false judgments in life. To be undeceived by disillusionment may leave us cynical and unkindly severe in our judgment of others, but the disillusionment, which comes from God brings us to the place where we see men and women as they really are, and yet there is no cynicism, we have no stinging, bitter things to say. Many of the cruel things in life spring from the fact that we suffer from illusions. We are not true to one another as facts; we are true only to our ideas of one another. Everything is either delightful and fine, or mean and dastardly, according to our idea.[23]

If you are living under the illusion of control, you must admit that many of the cruel things in life spring from the fact that you suffer from this warlord of waste. It is irrational to live under the spell of control, and even more insane that Christians refuse to disillusion themselves from it. Chambers continued:

The refusal to be disillusioned is the cause of much of the suffering in human life. It works in this way—if we love a human being and do not love God, we demand of him every perfection and every rectitude, and when we do not get it we become cruel and vindictive; we are demanding of a human being that which he or she cannot give. There is only one Being Who can satisfy the last aching abyss of the human heart, and that is the Lord Jesus Christ. Why Our Lord is apparently so severe regarding

---

[23] Oswald Chambers: "July 30th," in *My Utmost for His Highest* (New York, NY: Dodd, Mead & Company, 1935, repr. 1959), p. 212.

every human relationship is because He knows that every relationship not based on loyalty to Himself will end in disaster. Our Lord trusted no man, yet He was never suspicious, never bitter. Our Lord's confidence in God and in what His grace could do for any man, was so perfect that He despaired of no one. If our trust is placed in human beings, we shall end in despairing of everyone.[24]

We must put the warlord of control to death by embracing the sorrow of unmet longings and practicing the discipline of disillusionment. Since, however, the warlords of waste join forces, we must also refuse to allow regret to rule our intentions.

The Warlord of Regret

Are you ruled by regret? Whatever rules you is your lord. If regret has the predominant shaping influence in your life, Christ is not the object of your affections. What we regret reveals what we worship, and worship requires our affections. Affections affect our volitional strength, our intentionality for Christ.

Regret has a power over us in two ways. It rules people by keeping them hopeless about the future and unable to surrender the shattered dream of the past. In midlife we must slay this warlord of waste. Regret is caused by a loss so overwhelming, and sometimes so traumatic, that we do not know how to go on living. It may be a shattered hope or relationship. For example, divorce can be the occasion of regret. Dan Allender describes divorce this way:

---

[24] *Ibid.*

A divorce is an ending that just keeps churning up debris, a death that doesn't stop. ... The loss is so overwhelming that something in you does not know how to live and therefore keeps mourning, keeps being haunted by the loss itself.[25]

Divorce is a one-time event with ongoing effects that sends aftershocks relentlessly throughout a family. I attended a divorce recovery group years ago in seminary in order to shepherd adults who had experienced such a trauma. I participated in a group discussion, which enlightened me a good deal to this experience. One of the participants shared how he would miss his exit or destination because he dissociated while driving his car. Such grieving over loss required them to own what was, what is, and how to trust others in the future. It must be a grief surrendered, but it cannot have the final word. Dr. Allender offers this wise advice about the gospel intentionality required to slay the warlord of regret:

Bear the scar. Let the scar be a symbol, a reminder, an icon that you do bear the death of Christ, that he bears death for you. ... It isn't meant to say that this is a way to make positive merely the harm of the past. It's an intent to be able to say the resurrection wins, and no death, no divorce, no loss of dreams has a final command over who you are and who you are meant to be. ... Ruin and harm will not have the final word ... No death, no divorce, no loss of dreams has a final command over who you are meant to be.[26]

---

[25] Dan Allender, https://theallendercenter.org/2015/05/endings-4/
[26] *Ibid.*

Regret rules people whose intent is to refuse their powerlessness to fix what took place, to take it back, to undo it, or to change their past. Regret prompts us to push the replay button with an assumption that if only one small action had taken place, all this grief could have been avoided. Dwelling on regret like this, however, is a waste of time. Dr. Martin Lloyd-Jones in his book *Spiritual Depression* wrote:

> Let us then lay this down as a principle. We must never for a second worry about anything that cannot be affected or changed by us. It is a waste of energy ... You can sit down and be miserable and you can go round and round in circles of regret for the rest of your life but it will make no difference to what you have done.[27]

Lloyd Jones goes on to get his readers to turn away from themselves and to gaze at Christ. He believes that

> Part of the trouble with these people is that they are still morbidly preoccupied with themselves, that they have not learned as Christians that they are to deny self and take up the Cross and follow Him and to leave themselves, past present and future in His hands ... stop looking at yourself and begin to enjoy Him ... If you were to feel more interest in Christ you would be less interested in yourself. Begin to look at Him, gaze upon Him with this open, unveiled face. And then go on to learn that in His Kingdom what matters is not the length of

---

[27] David Martin Lloyd Jones, *Spiritual Depression* (London: HarperCollins, 1965), p. 82.

service but your attitude towards Him, your desire
to please Him.[28]

Slaying this warlord of waste is no easy matter, and it requires
gospel intentionality. Regret must not rule us; rather we pray that
God will hallow His name in tragedy and that His kingdom will
come rule over all our regrets. When William Borden of Yale College
was in Burma on his deathbed, dying prematurely in route to Cairo
for missions, he did not push the replay button to try to fix what
went wrong. He let God be God. The physicians around him were
also graduates of Yale, and felt differently. The doctors were saying
to themselves, "What a waste!" Borden groaned out his last words
on that deathbed, "No reserves; no retreats; no regrets."

The Warlord of Fear

Proverbs 28:1 says: "The wicked flee when no one is pursuing, but the
righteous are as bold as a lion." All fear is a flight response to what
threatens us. Evil aims to distort our perspective about the future
by inflating what we fear into giant-sized people or problems. If
what we fear rules us, then the warlord of waste rules us more than
the gospel. By "catastrophizing" the future and by distorting what
threatens us, we are not going to live with gospel intentionality. We
will not lean into the future with courageous hope. It is better to fail
in a cause that will ultimately succeed than to succeed in a cause that
will ultimately fail.

Fear is a strategy of flight: to cringe before something or
someone who might hurt me based on the perception that self-
preservation is a better choice than engagement. Dan Allender and
Tremper Longman describe the four distorting effects of fear as, first

---

[28] *Ibid.*, pp. 87–88.

of all, making us seem more accountable than we really are; second, viewing ourselves as weaker than we really are; third, inflating the threat larger than it or he or she really is; and finally, making people and possible events too big and God too small.[29] Theodore Roosevelt, former US president, wrote:

> It is not the critic who counts; not the man who points out how the strong man stumbles, or where the doer of deeds could have done them better. The credit belongs to the man who is actually in the arena, whose face is marred by dust and sweat and blood; who strives valiantly; who errs, who comes short again and again, because there is no effort without error and shortcoming; but who does actually strive to do the deeds; who knows great enthusiasms, the great devotions; who spends himself in a worthy cause; who at the best knows in the end the triumph of high achievement, and who at the worst, if he fails, at least fails while daring greatly, so that his place shall never be with those cold and timid souls who neither know victory nor defeat.[30]

Courage is required to defeat fear in the battle for our affections for Christ. Am I willing to risk in order to gain by faith, hope, and love more joy in God for myself and others? Joab exhorted King David's army, saying: "Be of good courage, and let us be courageous

---

[29] Dan Allender and Tremper Longman III, *The Cry of The Soul: How Our Emotions Reveal Our Deepest Questions About God* (Colorado Springs, CO: Navpress, 1994), p. 88.

[30] Excerpt from the speech "Citizenship In A Republic" delivered at the Sorbonne, in Paris, France, on 23 April, 1910.

for our people, and for the cities of our God, and may the LORD do what seems good to him" (2 Samuel 10:12).

Esther acted courageously when she requested that her uncle:

> Go, gather all the Jews to be found in Susa, and hold a fast on my behalf, and do not eat or drink for three days, night or day. I and my young women will also fast as you do. Then I will go to the king, though it is against the law, and if I perish, I perish. (Esther 4:15–16)

Courage comes from the Lord and frees us from being ruled by this warlord of waste; namely, fear. G. K. Chesterton described how courage does this. He wrote:

> Take the case of courage. No quality has ever so much addled the brains and tangled the definitions of merely rational sages. Courage is almost a contradiction in terms. It means a strong desire to live taking the form of a readiness to die. 'He that will lose his life, the same shall save it,' is not a piece of mysticism for saints and heroes. It is a piece of everyday advice for sailors or mountaineers. It might be printed in an Alpine guide or a drill book. This paradox is the whole principle of courage; even of quite earthly or brutal courage. A man cut off by the sea may save his life if we will risk it on the precipice.
>
> He can only get away from death by continually stepping within an inch of it. A soldier surrounded by enemies, if he is to cut his way out, needs to combine a strong desire for living with a strange

carelessness about dying. He must not merely cling to life, for then he will be a coward, and will not escape. He must not merely wait for death, for then he will be a suicide, and will not escape. He must seek his life in a spirit of furious indifference to it; he must desire life like water and yet drink death like wine. No philosopher, I fancy, has ever expressed this romantic riddle with adequate lucidity, and I certainly have not done so. But Christianity has done more: it has marked the limits of it in the awful graves of the suicide and the hero, showing the distance between him who dies for the sake of living and him who dies for the sake of dying.[31]

What would your life look like if you desired life like water and drank death like wine? Go back to God and recapture your identity in Christ and your sense of calling, and arouse your affections for Christ. Courageous acts of ordinary kindness await you in your future, and they have eternal consequences.

Howard Hendricks tells the story of how years ago he took part in a Sunday school convention at Moody Memorial Church in Chicago. During a lunch break, three of his colleagues who were teaching at the convention walked across the street to a little hamburger shop. The place was filled, but soon a table for four opened up. They saw an elderly lady whom they knew was attending the convention because of the bag she was carrying, and they asked her to join them.

They learned she was eighty-three and from a town in Michigan's Upper Peninsula. In a church with a Sunday school of only sixty-five people, she taught a class of thirteen junior-high boys. She had

---

[31] Gilbert K. Chesterton, *Orthodoxy* (New York, NY: John Lane Company, 1908), p. 170.

traveled by Greyhound bus all the way to Chicago the night before the convention. Hendricks asked her why.

> In her words, "To learn something that would make me a better teacher." I thought at the time, Most people who had a class of thirteen junior-high boys in a Sunday school of only sixty-five would be breaking their arms to pat themselves on the back: "Who, me? Go to a Sunday school convention? I could teach it myself!" But not this woman.

> Eighty-four boys who sat under her teaching are now young men in full-time vocational ministry. Twenty-two are graduates of the seminary where I teach.

> If you were to ask me the secret to this woman's impact, I'd give you a totally different answer today from what I would have said thirty years ago. Back then I'd have credited her methodology.

> Now I believe it was because of her passion to communicate.[32]

The Warlord of Busyness

A frenetic busyness haunts many in the West. There is a milieu of busyness mixed with a subterranean love of the world that threatens to waste our life in this season of spiritual formation (1 John 2:15–16). Busyness is a refusal to make decisions and become intentional

---

[32] Howard Hendricks, *Teaching to Change Lives: Seven Proven Ways to Make Your Teaching Come Alive*, p. 15.

with one's life for Christ's sake. In a way, it is a form of laziness or procrastination.

The parable of the rich fool in Luke 12:13–21 shows how a man busied himself for ample goods, laying up comforts for himself in order to maximize pleasure and minimize pain. He is a description of a hedonist in the USA, who takes little pleasure in God nor suffers to be rich toward God. Jesus said: "So is the one who lays up treasure for himself and is not rich toward God." However busy the rich fool in this parable was, he was lazy in midlife because he refused to suffer with gospel intentionality in order to cultivate gospel transformation in the garden of relationships.[33]

Busy Being Undecided

A debate with Jesus began when an Old Testament scholar brings up an old chestnut; namely, a repeated and tedious debate about the 613 commands of God in the scriptures at that time. Which one was the most important? Jesus cited two in Deuteronomy 6 and Leviticus 19. Jesus answered,

> You shall love the Lord your God with all your heart and with all your soul and with all your mind. This is the great and first commandment. And a second is like it: You shall love your neighbor as yourself. On these two commandments depend all the scriptures. (Matthew 22:37–40)

The scholar was overwhelmed because he understood that every command was motivated and practiced by perfect love. He

---

[33] Busyness is a form of laziness. See Genesis 2–3; Proverbs 21:25–26; 22:13; 24:10–12; 24:30–34; 26:13–16.

responded, therefore, saying that all the burnt offerings in the world would not be sufficient to make up for the human deficiencies in loving well, let alone perfectly.

Jesus, gladdened by the scholar's response, said: "You are not far from the kingdom of God" (Mark 12:34). This man made progress because he saw he needed Christ's righteousness and death to pardon his sins. We are halfway to heaven when we admit we are not saved, but we are still not all the way until we receive the free gift of salvation by faith alone. This is when busyness and lazy procrastination can hinder our intentionality for Christ.

There once was a dear man in this condition—too busy and lacking intentionality. One Sunday night he went to church, and God spoke to him through the sermon. Christ was striving with him that night. The pastor invited people to meet with him in his office to receive the free gift of eternal life.

The service finished, and out he went on his way back home. Sliding down the row, walking out the aisle, pushing open the doors, and marching along the sidewalk, he found himself unable to walk out the gates. He suddenly turned. He went marching back along the sidewalk, pushing open the doors, and walking up the aisle. As he was approaching the pastor's office door, he was struck with the thought, *This is crazy.* So he went back out the church, walking out down the aisle, pushing open the doors, marching along the sidewalk, and finding himself unable to step through the gates. He suddenly turned back.

This went on for two or three times while a church officer was tending the gates and watching this guy. The man looked, to the officer, like a man pursued by an unseen being. That is because he was. The officer said to him, "Listen, you really will need to make up your mind. Is it going to be *in* or *out*? I am shutting these doors and gates soon." And the man, who was not far from the kingdom of God, replied, "By God's grace it will be *in*!"

The officer at the gate is Jesus, and you may be the one not far from his kingdom. Jesus says to you today: "Listen, you really will need to make up your mind. Is it going to be *in* or *out*? I am soon shutting these gates." You better at least come to the point where you are prepared to say like the man, who was not far from the kingdom, in reply: "By God's grace it will be *in!*"

Hedonism, seeking to maximize pleasure and minimize pain, is adding to the cause of busyness because so much information is before our minds. The massive amount of social media information and images today requires us to intentionally steward what we allow into our minds. Will we process so much informational imaging well? Is it profitable? Does it cause us to stumble? Is it edifying? Does it glorify God? Neil Postman may sound like a neo-Luddite, (one opposed to technology), but he warns against amusing ourselves to death in an image culture that no longer reads and meditates upon deep truths about life. *Amuse* literally means to not think or muse. Postman wrote:

> What is happening in America is that television is transforming all serious public business into junk … Television disdains exposition, which is serious, sequential, rational, and complex. It offers instead a mode of discourse in which everything is accessible, simplistic, concrete, and above all, entertaining. As a result, America is the world's first culture in jeopardy of amusing itself to death.[34]

Busyness and Laziness each cry out, "I am a victim!" They claim, "I am entitled to receive rescue and rest!" If Busyness angrily says, "You owe me credit and rescue for all I do!" Laziness, then, fearfully says, "I deserve an easier life. I can't make a decision to risk

---

[34] Neil Postman, *Amusing Ourselves to Death: Public Discourse in the Age of Show Business* (New York, NY: Penguin Books, 1985), pp. 15–18.

eliminating all these things in my life! Besides, there is a dangerous lion out there!" Both are resigned to live under the warlord of busyness because they complain about how they do not have enough time or resources to live intentionally for Christ. In midlife people complain of overwork and busyness. Charles Swindoll wrote about a middle aged and overworked individual who was sure he was the only one working hard. Swindoll wrote:

> YES, I'M TIRED. For several years I've been blaming it on middle age, iron poor blood, lack of vitamins, air pollution, water pollution, saccharin, obesity, dieting, underarm odor, yellow wax buildup, and a dozen other maladies that make you wonder if life is really worth living. But now I find out, tain't that. I'm tired because I'm overworked.
>
> The population of this country is over 200 million. Eighty-four million are retired. That leaves 116 million to do the work. There are 75 million in school, which leaves 41 million to do the work. Of this total, there are 22 million employed by the government. That leaves 19 million to do the work. Four million are in the armed forces, which leaves 15 million to do the work. Take from that total the 14,800,000 people who work for the state and city governments and that leaves 200,000 to do the work. There are 188,000 in hospitals, so that leaves 12,000 to do the work. Now there are 11,998 people in prisons. That leaves just 2 people to do the work. You and me. And you're standing there reading this. No wonder I'm tired.[35]

[35] Swindoll, Charles (1998-11-20). The Tale of the Tardy Oxcart (Swindoll Leadership Library) (p. 319). Thomas Nelson. Kindle Edition.

Limitations and Margins

Busyness can be a slow death. Henri Nouwen, in saying it was a way to spiritual death, wrote:

> Aren't you, like me, hoping that some person, thing, or event will come along to give you that final feeling of inner well-being you desire? Don't you often hope: 'May this book, idea, course, trip, job, country or relationship fulfill my deepest desire.' But as long as you are waiting for that mysterious moment you will go on running helter-skelter, always anxious and restless, always lustful and angry, never fully satisfied. You know that this is the compulsiveness that keeps us going and busy, but at the same time makes us wonder whether we are getting anywhere in the long run. This is the way to spiritual exhaustion and burn-out. This is the way to spiritual death.[36]

Moses is often a model for leadership, especially in the ways that he learns from his mistakes that mirror our own. One of his first lessons in leadership was to live within God-set limits or margins. The first sign that Moses had no margins in his life was when Moses sent the wife and children to Grandpa's home so he could keep up with work. Jethro must have been happy to spend time with little Gershom and his daughter, Zipporah. A message was being sent, however, that Moses' work might not have been compatible for his wife and children.

Later when Grandpa came to spend some holiday time with

---

[36] Henri J. M. Nouwen, *Life of the Beloved* (Wheaton, IL: Crossway Books, 2007), p. 35. Kindle Edition.

Moses, he saw Moses' blind spot again. Moses defensively replied, "The people come to me … they come to me, and I …" His father-in-law, however, replied: "What you are doing is not good. You and the people with you will certainly wear yourselves out, for the thing is too heavy for you" (Exodus 18:15–18). In the words of author Richard Swenson:

> When you reach the limits of your resources or abilities, you have no margin left. Yet because we don't even know what margin is, we don't realize it is gone … Our pain is palpable, but our assailant remains unnamed.[37]

Limits must be faced or crashed into like a brick wall. Our space, time, and body's energy each inform us that there are limits to our relational capacity, season in life, and calling that require us to choose either contentment or the consequences of pushing the limits. Surely you cannot be more than one person who is needed in your own family and community. Learning to rest and trust God's acceptance of your limits is a step of progress towards intentional living for Christ.

The Gospel is our Greatest Spiritual Weapon

How shall we engage in spiritual warfare and slay these dragons, these warlords of waste? Only the gospel has the power with the Spirit to transform the heart, defeat evil, and raise our affections in accord with holy intentions. Justified self-entitlements to

---

[37] Richard A. Swenson, *Margin: Restoring Emotional, Physical, Financial, and Time Reserves to Overloaded Lives* (Colorado Springs, CO: Navpress, 2004) Kindle Edition, p. 18; location 472.

unchallenged busyness, laziness, cowardice, controlling strategies, or regret-ruled attitudes and behaviors must be dismantled and proven foolish towards obtaining a future and a gospel-written life story we all were meant to enjoy. In the next chapter we will consider gospel repentance, faith, and healing.

Misplaced affections are the delight of the evil one. Evil is content to let us exchange an old affection with a new one, as long as your affections are still misplaced. A young teen can idolize pleasure and exchange his affection for another idol of wealth. He may have appeared rebellious in his youth and moral in his twenties, but his heart lacks vital affections for Christ expressed by gospel intentionality. The only solution, in the words of Thomas Chalmers, is "the explosive power of a new one"—namely, a new and explosive affection for Christ. He wrote:

> The love of God and the love of the world, are two affections, not merely in a state of rivalship, but in a state of enmity—and that so irreconcilable, that they cannot dwell together in the same bosom. We have already affirmed how impossible it were for the heart, by any innate elasticity of its own, to cast the world away from it; and thus reduce itself to a wilderness. The heart is not so constituted; and the only way to dispossess it of an old affection, is by the expulsive power of a new one. The heart is so constituted, and the only way to dispossess it of an old affection is by the explosive power of a new one.[38]

---

[38] Thomas Chalmers, sermon: "The Explosive Power of A New Affection" found on Monergism's website: https://www.monergism.com/thethreshold/ sdg/Chalmers,%20Thomas%20-%20The%20Exlpulsive%20Power%20of%20 a%20New%20Af.pdf

Discussion Group Questions:

1. Are there legions of evil warlords of waste? Perhaps, but these four are common to those in midlife. Which one(s) attempt to waste your life most at this time?

2. A warlord of waste is anything that occupies God's place, anything that drives your life, any substitute that you trust will make you happier and that determines your behavior. We are called to continually root all of these out of our lives. To do this, you must first discern them and become utterly ruthless with yourself in asking the questions:

   • *Is there anything other than God that is driving my life and causing me to do things, that are contrary to God's commandments or become the false motivation to keep His commandments?*

   • *Is there anything besides God that I believe I must have in order to be happy?*

3. Here are three questions about busyness and living within the limits:

   Am I living within the limits of who you are—as an individual and family and community?

   Am I living within the limits of what I have been called to do—not what others are called to do?

   Am I living and giving my best within the limits of the place where I have been given to serve—trusting God to enlarge my sphere of influence and belonging if and when I am ready?

Chapter 3

Gospel Transformation at Midlife:
Repentance, Healing, and Faith

Our Greatest Weapon

There is nothing more than the gospel needed for the fight, but there is sure a lot more of the gospel to equip us for the fight. We can declare independence from our tendencies to want to control everything and others. We can free ourselves from the rule of regrets in our past, from inordinate fears, and from busyness. The gospel offers us transformation when we repent, rest in Christ, and heal through the Holy Spirit. The gospel promises us freedom to intentionally risk for Christ's sake, but we must trust its veracity. The gospel is the *hors d'oeurve* that wins us to salvation, the milk that young Christians scream for in order to grow, and the meat for the mature to become strong in the Lord. The gospel is the milk and the meat for all four seasons of spiritual formation.

Gospel Repentance

A common experience in midlife is losing heart—your first love. The Church in Ephesus was told by Christ:

I know you are enduring patiently and bearing up
for My Name's sake, and you have grown weary.
But I have this against you that you have abandoned
the love you had at first. Remember therefore from
where you have fallen; repent, and do the works you
did at first. (Revelation 2: 3-5)

When we lose heart, we lose intentionality. When affections for
God are raised again, gospel intentionality increases.

Paul describes his sorrow over the Christians in Galatia, who
began to base their acceptance with God upon their performance
rather than on the performance of Christ on their behalf, addressing
them as "[m]y little children, for whom I am again in the anguish of
childbirth until Christ is formed in you." (Galatians 4:19) Spiritual
formation began well as they found their identity in Christ, but came
to a halt when the gospel was seen as only a way of salvation in the
beginning of the Christian life. Gospel repentance, then, is the key
to ongoing spiritual formation in every season of the Christian life.

Gospel repentance is not legal repentance. The former begins
with the joy of acceptance and leads to spiritual life. The latter begins
with condemnation and self-hatred, leading to spiritual death. If the
warlords of waste describe you, then you are a candidate for grace.
There is not one objection a Christian can raise against him or
herself for why God should not love him or her. God is the Father of
the humble, miserable, and desperate. It is God's nature to exalt the
humble, to forgive the chief of sinners, to heal the wounded, to feed
the hungry, and to justify the unrighteous as righteous in His sight.
It is the kindness of God that welcomes us home and celebrates our
return. The way of repentance safely directs us on the path as restful
pilgrims again. As Eugene Peterson put it, repentance is:

Deciding that you have been wrong in supposing
that you could manage your own life and be your

own god; it is deciding that you were wrong in thinking that you had, or could get, the strength, education and training to make it on your own; it is deciding that you have been told a pack of lies about yourself and your neighbours and your world. And it is deciding that God, in Jesus Christ, is telling you the truth. Repentance is a realisation that what God wants from you and what you want from God are not going to be achieved by doing the same old things, thinking the same old thoughts. Repentance is a decision to follow Jesus Christ and become his pilgrim in the path of peace.[39]

How we view God makes all the difference in our repentance; whether we view him as a tyrant or a loving Father determines whether we are attempting legalistic repentance or gospel repentance. Charles H. Spurgeon wrote:

While I regarded God as a tyrant I thought my sin a trifle; But when I knew Him to be my Father, then I mourned that I could ever have kicked against Him. When I thought God was hard, I found it easy to sin; but when I found God so kind, so good, so overflowing with compassion, I smote upon my breast to think that I could ever have rebelled against One who loved me so, and sought my good.[40]

Gospel repentance comes to us when we not only see Him as He truly is, but also when we know He is looking at us. He sees right

---

[39] Eugene H. Peterson, *A Long Obedience in the Same Direction* (Downers Grove, IL: InterVarsity Press, 1980), pp. 246–2477.

[40] Charles H. Spurgeon, "Repentance after Conversion," Sermon, No. 2419, June 12, 1887.

through us without condemnation, but with compassion and mercy. It is the kindness of God that leads to repentance. Paul asked: "Or do you presume on the riches of his kindness and forbearance and patience, not knowing that God's kindness is meant to lead you to repentance?" (Romans 2:4). John Calvin described when Jesus turned and looked at Peter after Peter's third denial and the rooster's crowing. Calvin wrote:

> When Christ looked at Peter, he added the secret power of the Spirit to his eyes, so that, by the rays of his grace, his look penetrated into Peter's very heart. From this let us know that when a man falls he will not even begin to repent, unless the Lord look at him.[41]

Gospel repentance engages and raises our spiritual affections for Christ because He has brought us to the Father, who loves us. It is a matter of rejoicing in Christ rather than fearing Christ's displeasure in us. Timothy Keller writes about the importance of holy affections for Christ in repentance. His understanding of gospel repentance differs from fear-based repentance. He writes:

> Rejoicing and repentance must go together. Repentance without rejoicing will lead to despair. Rejoicing without repentance is shallow and will only provide passing inspiration instead of deep change. Indeed, it is when we rejoice over Jesus' sacrificial love for us most fully that, paradoxically, we are most truly convicted of our sin. When we

---

[41] John Calvin, *Commentary on A Harmony of the Evangelists, Matthew, Mark, and Luke* (Grand Rapids, MI: Baker Book House, reprint 1993), Volume 27, p. 265.

repent out of fear of consequences, we are not really sorry for the sin, but for ourselves.

Fear-based repentance (I'd better change or God will get me) is really self-pity. In fear-based repentance, we don't learn to hate the sin for itself, and it doesn't lose its attractive power. We learn only to refrain from it for our own sake. But when we rejoice over God's sacrificial, suffering love for us—seeing what it cost Him to save us from sin—we learn to hate the sin for what it is. We see what the sin cost God. What most assures us of God's unconditional love (Jesus' costly death) is what most convicts us of the evil of sin. Fear-based repentance makes us hate ourselves. Joy-based repentance makes us hate the sin.[42]

Gospel Healing

When we lose heart, we experience disintegration. Restoring an integrated heart is a work of the Spirit of grace, a healing work. Throughout the reliable history of redemption, the Bible reveals how the gospel brought healing to saints whose dreams and relationships had been shattered in midlife.

Abraham and Sarah, for example, were ready to throw in the towel and give up on having the promised child, but God relentlessly reminded them of His promise to the point where they laughed. They dreamed of their lives going a certain way, and they tried to fulfill it themselves when they had Ishmael. When their son was born to them in old age, they named him *Isaac*, which means laughter. God

---

[42] Timothy J. Keller, *Counterfeit Gods: The Empty Promise of Money, Sex, and Power and the Only Hope that Matters* (New York, NY: Dutton, 2009), 172.

healed their hearts. Subsequently, Abraham was called to sacrifice his son as a test of who had supremacy in his life. Each saint's story mirrored the Bible's metanarrative: there was an initial experience of happiness followed by a fall. This was followed up with a promise of redemption, which led to healing and restoration in the end. Where are you in the gospel narrative?

In a very real sense midlife is the experience of a shattered dream. Paul David Tripp is certain that we will dream. He describes a dream:

> A dream is imagination coupled with desire projected into the future ... We are creatures of dreams, whether they might be realistic and out of reach or not ... We all carry a vision in our heart ... Maybe it isn't clear at the present time, but it is indeed very much alive and waiting for you to discover. This vision carries us through life and motivates *us*.[43]

After the initial dream, as it were, is given birth, we experience the fall. We over-edit the dream with our imaginations until we are no longer living for Christ, but rather for the dream. Tripp argues that our dreams will either die or disappoint us. He continues:

> The more I replay my dream, the more detailed it gets and the more it has control of me. Each day that I work, I am a person in pursuit of a dream. Before long the dream is not just a faint and distant hope for the future. It becomes a prized possession. I become convinced that life without that dream

---

[43] Paul David Tripp, *Lost in the Middle—MidLife and the Grace of God* (Wapwallopen, PA: Shepherd Press, 2004), pp. 144–147.

would be unthinkable and unlivable. My sense of identity, purpose, well-being, contentment, and satisfaction becomes directly connected to the realization of the dream. My imagination has been captured and is now controlled by some aspect of the creation. It was never meant to be that way. All other dreams were meant to be subservient to God's dream. Yet in the pursuit of my essential dream, I have been slowly building my own personal tower to my own personal heaven. It has me. It motivates me. It guides and directs me ... Yesterday's dream becomes today's demand. Today's demand morphs into tomorrow's needs. What once got my attention has now become the thing that I cannot live without. Remember this dream principle: the dream for a good thing becomes a bad thing when that dream becomes a ruling thing. This is the danger of our dreams.[44]

Tripp argues:

A dream does not fulfill you; it never did and it never will. It doesn't give you an identity nor an emotional security. It won't give you this sense of meaning and purpose that you are actually seeking to get. How many people have fulfilled their dreams, only to feel empty, hungry, and lost once more?[45]

When our dreams are shattered, we need gospel healing. Larry Crabb wrote: "Shattered dreams are not accidents of fate. They

---

[44] *Ibid.*

[45] *Ibid.*

are ordained opportunities for the Spirit first to awaken, then to satisfy our higher dream."[46] When we experience gospel healing, we are comforted by God's plan for our lives. Our plans, then, fall into line with His, giving integration, congruity, and contentment inside and out of our lives. Internally, the Holy Spirit is forming your integrity in Christ in order that an outward expression of Christ's advancement of His kingdom might be made through you on the earth. This requires gospel metamorphous and transformation—an integration of inward and outward congruity with His will for your life. The scriptures teach that the renewing of our minds leads us into is a more reliable process of discernment. "Do not be conformed to this world, but be transformed by the renewal of your mind, that by testing you may discern what is the will of God, what is good and acceptable and perfect" (Romans 12:2).

Midlife is not only an experience of shattered dreams, but also shattered relationships that need gospel healing. In transitional periods of life, like "half-time" in the contest of life, you can benefit from a healing process of reintegrating polarities in your life—young and old, attachment and separation, and gentleness and strength—especially, your sense of your dependence and independence within community and family. More importantly, restoring shattered relationships is a central concern in the gospel healing process. Our relational brokenness will either keep us too dependent on others, or it will keep us too independent from them.

Two pitfalls that may have led to a shattering of your relationships that need healing are relational fusion and relational exclusion. Relational fusion is an idea that comes from a description of two metals losing their identities when melted. To the degree a healthy separation from an enmeshed relationship takes place, healing may take place. Without a healthy and holy separation from others, we

---

[46] Larry Crabb, *Shattered Dreams: God's Unexpected Pathway to Joy* (Colorado Springs, CO: WaterBrook Press, 2001), p. 5.

tend to lose the freedom necessary to express godly intentionality. This pitfall is also called enmeshment. Henri Nouwen described the effects on a person enmeshed with others when he wrote:

> As long as I keep running about asking: "Do you love me? Do you really love me?" I give all power to the voices of the world and put myself in bondage because the world is filled with "ifs." The world says: "Yes, I love you if you are good-looking, intelligent, and wealthy. I love you if you have a good education, a good job, and good connections. I love you if you produce much, sell much, and buy much." There are endless "ifs" hidden in the world's love. These "ifs" enslave me, since it is impossible to respond adequately to all of them. The world's love is and always will be conditional. As long as I keep looking for my true self in the world of conditional love, I will remain "hooked" to the world—trying, failing, and trying again. It is a world that fosters addictions because what it offers cannot satisfy the deepest craving of my heart.[47]

Besides relational fusion, relational exclusion is a pitfall in community living. Relational exclusion describes a differentiation process of an individual from others, which has gone too far. It is an exaggeration of one's need to be separate. This imbalance in relationships is a sign that the person is trying to maintain an illusion of a secure identity above and against others. This person may be letting a relational wound keep you from coming present to

---

[47]   Henri J. M. Nouwen, *The Return of the Prodigal Son*, (New York, NY: Penguin Random House, 1992), pp. 49–50.

others. Until the wound is healed with gospel wisdom and love the person is less volitional and more governed by the wound.

Healing can take place wonderfully in a spiritual formation group when the leader gives pause to the discussion for the sake of asking the healing balm of the gospel and the Holy Spirit to make the group members sound and healthy again.

As the Holy Spirit powerfully heals and puts together our disintegrated and incongruous lives, which are enmeshed with relational fusion and weakened by relational exclusion, the Christian in midlife must face risking for a better future. John Gayner Banks wrote:

> Cast aside the last vestage of unbelief and embrace that destiny, which you feared to accept on account of your limit … those hardships are now transcended by the might of My indwelling Spirit.[48]

When we have experienced gospel repentance and gospel healing, we are ready to trust the good news and live intentionally in the context of community without enmeshment to another or in isolation. The gospel announces the good news that we are forgiven, healing, and saved from shattered dreams and relationships. When we trust it, then we take intentional risks for Christ.

Gospel Faith

Although God never risks, we do.

The Jewish people were in exile; the setting was Babylon and the king was Nebuchadnezzar. He set up an image of gold, and

---

[48] John Gaynor Banks, *The Master and the Disciple* (St. Paul, MN: Macalaster Park Publishing, 1954), p. 22.

then commanded that when the trumpet sounded, all the people should bow down to the image. Shadrach, Meshach, and Abednego did not bow down. They worshiped the one true God of Israel. So Nebuchadnezzar threatened them and said that if they did not worship the image, they would be thrown into the fiery furnace. When Shadrach, Meshach, and Abednego were asked by the king if there was a god who would deliver them out of the fiery furnace, they said to the king:

> O Nebuchadnezzar, we have no need to answer you in this matter. If this be so, our God whom we serve is able to deliver us from the burning fiery furnace, and he will deliver us out of your hand, O king. But if not, be it known to you, O king, that we will not serve your gods or worship the golden image that you have set up. (Daniel 3:16-18)

Satan's subtle strategies play on our sinful strategies to avoid taking risks necessary during this season of intentionality. By trusting God's favor over us in Christ, we are made willing to take steps of faith to make our greatest contributions in this season of spiritual formation like Daniel's friends in the Lord. Oswald Sanders in *Spiritual Leadership* reminded us that four major poets over the age of eighty did most their best work in the last decade of their lives than in their twenties and thirties. Chuck Swindoll wrote:

> William Gladstone took up a new language when he was seventy, and at eighty-three he became the prime Minister of Great Britain—for the fourth time. At eighty-three! Alfred Lloyd Tennyson wrote Crossing the Bar when he was eighty. John Wesley was eighty-eight and still preaching daily with eminent success, eloquent power, and

undiminished popularity. At eighty-eight! Every day! Michelangelo painted his world famous The Last Judgment when he was sixty-six.[49]

Two false notions keep us from taking risks for Christ by faith. The first is the notion that says: "I must wait and never initiate in a way that appears proud. Who am I to think I can _____?" This exposes that we are not embracing our identity in Christ, and that the humble thing to do is to stay conventional and blend into the herd. The second is the false notion that says: "God has not blessed me like others, who simply had more opportunities and blessings than me. I must surrender to injustice. Life is not fair, but I choose to suffer humbly as a victim." This notion exposes our justification for not trusting God and the gospel. Since you are in Christ, you are not a victim. Since you are not a victim, there is no justification for remaining stuck in self-pity and envy. You and I must risk, even when we pray. Henri Nouwen wrote that praying

> Demands that you take to the road again and again, leaving your house and looking forward to a new land for yourself and your [fellow human]. This is why praying demands poverty, that is, the readiness to live a life in which you have nothing to lose so that you always begin afresh.[50]

The gospel offers us transformation when we repent, receive healing from shattered dreams and relationships, and place our trust in the truth of the gospel by taking risks for Christ. In the next

---

[49] Charles Swindoll, *Living on the Ragged Edge: Finding Joy in a World Gone Mad* (Nashville, TN: Thonas Nelson, 2007), p. 321. See also Oswald Sanders, *Spiritual Leadership* (Chicago, IL: Moody Press, 1967, repr. 1972).

[50] Henri J. M. Nouwen, *With Open Hands* (Notre Dame, IN: Ave Maria Press, 1972, repr. 2006), p. 147.

chapter we will explore our stories to discern how God converging both our experiences and callings in a way that will make us more intentional for Christ.

Discussion Group Questions:

1. What is the God-given essence of your calling in which you come most alive?
2. What activities would you prefer to eliminate doing each week, month, or year?
3. When have you been most fruitful in gospel service? Who was instrumental? What was your role?
4. Are you so fused with another that you cannot seem to express godly and earnest intentions for your future unless the other person has the same ones as you?
5. Have you become too independent from your family and community so that you find yourself thinking less of others?
6. What risks ought to be taken in faith in order to invest your spiritual and financial endowments, experience, and skills in a way that fully expresses your God-given passion into the lives of others for the next decade?

Chapter 4

The Convergence of Experience and Grace

God is converging everything from our past in order to shape us for the future. He is inviting us to raise our affection for Christ and to overcome the warlords of waste for a better day. In this chapter we will consider the convergence of our experience and God's grace to us in our gospel stories.

One day we shall behold Christ with incredible happiness, which we can hardly imagine. We have five senses now, but one day we may have a thousand, and every sense shall be satisfied in seeing Christ. Jonathan Edwards's sermon on 1 John 3:2, "And it does not yet appear what we shall be" points to the happiness in Christ that awaits every Christian. His main point: "The godly are designed for unknown and inconceivable happiness." Edwards wrote:

> [The] glory of God [does not] consist merely in the creature's perceiving his perfections: for the creature may perceive the power and wisdom of God, and yet take no delight in it, but abhor it. Those creatures that so do, don't glorify God. Nor doth the glory of God consist especially in speaking of his perfections: for words avail not any otherwise than as they express the sentiment of the mind.

This glory of God, therefore, [consists] in the creature's admiring and rejoicing [and] exulting in the manifestation of his beauty and excellency ... The essence of glorifying ... God consists, therefore, in the creature's rejoicing in God's manifestations of his beauty, which is the joy and happiness we speak of. So we see it comes to this at last: that the end of the creation is that God may communicate happiness to the creature; for if God created the world that he may be glorified in the creature, he created it that they might rejoice in his glory: for we have shown that they are the same.[51]

The Convergence of Experience and Grace in One's Gospel Story

Most people lack perspective when it comes to seeing the gospel story of their life. It is easy at times to live without a sense of God's overall involvement and shaping in your life. Arranging our life into chapters is a way to listen to the Author's message, and to begin to tell others His greater story. God's providence, His sustaining and ruling all things for His glory, will help you become intentional in this season of spiritual formation.

Our life reads, in a sense, like a story. There is a beginning, middle, and end. It consists of a plot, which has a tension moving towards a resolution. The Psalmist pictures God as an author when he said: "Your eyes saw my unformed substance; in your book were written, every one of them, the days that were formed for me, when as yet there was none of them" (Psalm 139:16).

God, we might say, has authored your redemptive story for you

---

[51] Jonathan Edwards, *Works (Yale)*, vol. 14, p. 144.

to listen with spiritual ears. Since He knows you and your story, He is more than willing to interpret for you through the lens of the bible and the Holy Spirit. The Psalmist goes on to say: "You know when I sit and when I rise; you perceive my thoughts from afar. You discern my going out and my lying down; you are familiar with all my ways" (Psalms 139:2–3).

Your life itself is a story in a story-craving culture, but there is a story-war over which your story will be heard; the gospel feast competes with the fast food stories of post-modernity. The chapters of your story can be wrongly interpreted.

Dr. Fuller, called "The Unity of the Bible" the unifying flag of God's mercy, is hoisted over the whole Bible. He sees the story nature in the Bible, when he wrote:

> God ordained a redemptive history whose sequence fully displays his glory so that, at the end, the greatest possible number of people would have had the historical antecedents necessary to engender [the most] fervent love for God ... The one thing God is doing in all of redemptive history is to show forth his mercy in such a way that the greatest number of people will throughout eternity delight in him with all their heart, strength, and mind ... When the earth of the new creation is filled with such people, then God's purpose in showing forth his mercy will have been achieved ... All the events of redemptive history and their meaning as recorded in the Bible compose a unity in that they conjoin to bring about this goal.[52]

---

[52] Daniel Fuller, *The Unity of the Bible: Unfolding God's Plan for Humanity* (Grand Rapids, Mich.: Zondervan, 1992), pp. 453–454.

God's story, the Bible, has four main chapters to its meta-narrative.[53] The first is Eden. Start by asking yourselves what the moments of shalom (peace) and happiness were in your early years? Who were the people that were a waft of heaven? What were the places that seemed like Eden? It is similar to how a story like "Cinderella" begins. There is a happy daughter who is loved by her father and mother.

The second chapter is the fall; namely, tragedy. This is when Eden was lost and shalom was shattered. In Cinderella's life it was when her mother died, her father married her cruel stepmother, two spoiled step sisters lived in her home, and her father subsequently died. In the Old Testament there are three primary types of people who experience tragedy the most in life east of Eden. These are orphans, strangers (aliens), and widows. From this chapter we may ask about the second chapter of our lives, when did we experience a loss of guidance and support? When did we suffer loss of friendship and estrangement? When did we loose a lover, and even begin to hate our looks or our bodies?

The third chapter is redemption and rescue. Here the tension of the plot thickens. This is when evil is threatened with the promise of redemption, and when hope begins to fill the heart of the rescued. In Cinderella's story, it was when there was a promise given by the king to marry the prince. It was the possibility of attending the ball and the magical rescue of a fairy. The prince falls in love with Cinderella, evil is exposed and punished justly, and she marries the prince. In chapter three of our lives we may ask how our story will reveal the gospel. When did we experience resolutions from the tension of the plot along the way? These chapter endings are denouements where complexities are resolved, where the tension relaxes a bit, and where

---

[53] Scotty Smith and Dan B. Allender have both influenced me with this perspective. Dan Allender, *To Be Told: Know Your Story, Shape Your Life* (Colorado Springs, CO: WaterBrook Press, 2005).

we experience a temporary rest. What were the places, moments, people involved in the denouements of our story?

The fourth and final chapter of the Bible, and for us, is the consummation. This is how our story will end in triumph over evil, when everything that has happened will converge into one fine day. What will it be like? How do you imagine evil facing judgment and life in the kingdom of Christ?

When we interpret life in this gospel way we have God's perspective, and we are fortified with both realism and hope to live the rest of our life with intentionality for Christ. Henri Nouwen wrote on the benefits of knowing and owning our life as God's story:

> The man who articulates the movements of his inner life, who can give names to his varied experiences, need no longer be a victim of himself, but is able slowly and consistently to remove the obstacles that prevent the spirit from entering. He is able to create space for Him whose heart is greater than his, whose eyes see more than his, and whose hands can heal more than his.[54]

Stories are revelatory to show how God creates beauty out of ashes. For us not to listen to them would be to ignore God's voice in a major way.

How to Capture Your Story in Four Steps

There is a very practical way to better understand your story in a way that leads to a convergence of your experience and God's grace in

---

[54] Henri J. M. Nouwen, *The Wounded Healer: Ministry in Contemporary Society* (New York, NY: Doubleday, 1972), p. 38.

your life. Since it is practical, it requires effort on your part (30–45 minutes).

Step 1 is to write down in the first column in the chart below significant events, people, and circumstances that describe your first chapter of life—Eden. Write a few words about each event or person that will sufficiently describe the impact of this experience. A goal would be to try and create as many as three to five of these entries. It is best if you work independently. Even if the most seemingly insignificant memories come to mind, go ahead and write them down. If they prove to be insignificant you can discard them later.

- People—Parents, grandparents, relatives, friends, ministry contacts, teachers, coaches, pastors, etc.
- Events—Holidays, vacations, visits, amusement parks, backyards, etc.
- Circumstances—Smells, places, creation, sounds, tastes, etc.
- Messages—Words, facial expressions, music, body language, etc.

Chapter 1	Chapter 2	Chapter 3	Chapter 4
1.			
2.			
3.			
4.			
5.			

In step 2, write down in the second column in chart below significant events, people, and circumstances that describe your second chapter of life—the fall. Not everything in life is positive, and these painful events recall when shalom was shattered and pain was authored in. Again describe the people, events, circum-stances, and messages that took you outside of your Eden. Ask yourself: when were you orphaned—when did you experience a loss of guidance and support? When were you alienated—when did you suffer loss of friendship and suffer estrangement from significant others? When were you widowed—when did you lose a lover and even begin to hate your looks or your body?

Step 3 is the chapter on redemption. Organize the God-important or kairotic moments in your story when God was redeeming the fall; when you experienced guidance and support; when you were included into meaningful fellowship; and when you were adored. Again describe the people, events, circumstances, and messages that transformed you with gospel hope (third column).

Finally, step 4 is about consummation. By looking back to the first chapter in your Eden, as it were, try to imagine how your story will end in heaven (column four). Heaven is described in Isaiah as an eschatological feast. Isaiah wrote of this feast in this way:

> On this mountain the LORD of hosts will make for
> all peoples
> a feast of rich food, a feast of well-aged wine,
> of rich food full of marrow,
> of aged wine well refined.
> And he will swallow up on this mountain
> the covering that is cast over all peoples,
> the veil that is spread over all nations.
> He will swallow up death forever;
> and the Lord GOD will wipe away tears from all faces,
> and the reproach of his people he will take away
> from all the earth,
> for the LORD has spoken.

> It will be said on that day,
> "Behold, this is our God; we have waited for him,
> that he might save us.
> This is the LORD; we have waited for him;
> let us be glad and rejoice in his salvation."
> (Isaiah 25:6-9)

Imagine through Isaiah's poetic genre what heaven will be like for you, then consider how you can be intentional for Christ in light of this one fine day.

The Convergence of Your Story and Personal Resolutions

A godly response to God's providence in your life will lead to personal resolutions. Jonathan Edwards, for example, did not waste his life. His first sermon at eighteen was an argument for why the Christian should be happy because everything bad will be used for good, everything good will never be taken away, and the best is yet to come.[55] Edwards's life ended abruptly from a failed smallpox vaccination when he was fifty-four, but he had lived with gospel intentionality. His life is inspiring because of his zeal not to waste his time. Consider some of the resolutions he wrote in his early twenties to intensify his life for the glory of God. Edwards wrote these when he was a young man. He wrote:

- Resolution #5: "Resolved, never to lose one moment of time; but improve it the most profitable way I possibly can."
- Resolution #6: "Resolved, to live with all my might, while I do live."

---

[55] Jonathan Edwards, *The Works of Jonathan Edwards* (New Haven, CT: Yale University Press, 1992), Volume 10, p. 294.

- Resolution #17: "Resolved, that I will live so, as I shall wish I had done when I come to die."
- Resolution #22: "Resolved, to endeavor to obtain for myself as much happiness, in the other world, as I possibly can, with all the power, might, vigor, and vehemence, yea violence, I am capable of, or can bring myself to exert, in any way that can be thought of."[56]

God is converging everything from our past in order to shape us for the future. He is inviting us to raise our affection for Christ and to overcome the warlords of waste for a better day. In this chapter we considered the convergence of our experience and God's grace to us in our gospel stories. We took time to practically record the four chapters of our story as they relate to the four chapters of the Bible. In the next chapter we will take time to write out our intentionality for Christ.

Discussion Group Questions:

1. Is there a connection or link from your experience of Eden and shalom, your experience of the fall and tragedy, to your experiences of redemption that points to a convergence at this point in your story?
2. Are your affections aroused to live more intentionally in light of God's commitment to redeem your worst experiences and to bring your story to a happy conclusion?
3. Prepare to share your intentionality for Christ by using the examples and the template provided in the next chapter.

---

[56] Jonathan Edwards, *The Works of Jonathan Edwards* (New Haven, CT: Yale University Press, 1998),Volume 16, pp. 753–759.

Chapter 5

This One Thing I Do

A Life of Cultivating Gospel Transformation

The apostle Paul said in Philippians,

> Brothers, I do not consider that I have made it my
> own. But one thing I do: forgetting what lies behind
> and straining forward to what lies ahead, I press on
> toward the goal for the prize of the upward call of
> God in Christ Jesus. (Philippians 3:13–14)

Obviously, Paul did many things, but they could be summarized under one heading. He was living intentionally for Christ by a life of gospel transformation, and he was committed to cultivating gospel transformation in others.

My first time leading an intentionality spiritual formation group in my church was in 2007. At the end of the six weekly meetings, I wrote out my gospel intentions for the next five years. One of them, now ten years later, was to train pastors globally because they have few resources. Since I have a PhD on Jonathan Edwards and had served in ministry in a variety of ways, I was a candidate. I'll never forget what I aimed for—two trips annually. What if I would have thought, "I'll wait until I am retired and old?" By then, I would be physically less able and have only made it to a few nations. Now, as of 2017, I have been to over twenty-five nations teaching pastors, leaders, and seminary students in a variety of theological subjects. I have preached in many churches and evangelized in many homes. What's my point? Taking time in this season to become intentional will save us from postponing life to our latter years— years when friends of mine in their fifties and sixties are suffering from unexpected afflictions.

As you write yours out, perhaps you would take time to listen to and meditate on the lyrics by Andrew Peterson's "Planting Trees." His lyrics describe the process of roots growing deep and branches spreading out "to bless the dawn" from just laying maples in a hole in the ground. Peterson compares them to children becoming adults that bless others through the years of a mother's loving prayers. Many years later after we are long gone, what we planted remains.

> So sit down and write that letter
> Sign up and join the fight
> Sink in to all that matters
> Step out into the light
>
> Let go of all that's passing
> Lift up the least of these
> Lean into something lasting
> Planting trees, hmm, yeah.[57]

---

[57] Andrew Peterson, "Planting Trees" in *Counting Stars* album released through Centricity Music on July 27, 2010.

Sharing My Intentionality for Christ

Please take time to review the following two templates from the first two seasons of spiritual formation (Appendix). If you can fill out your identity in Christ and your sense of calling to Christ, then it may help you clarify the template for this season of spiritual formation; namely, My intentionality for Christ.

Write out your intentionality for Christ and be prepared to share the following:

My Intentionality for Christ

As I came to grips with the common challenges of midlife, I have been confronted with how intentional the evil trinity (worldliness, the sinful nature, and the demonic kingdom) is for me to waste this season of spiritual formation—a season when I am able to make the greatest gospel contribution for Christ.

I have identified the following "warlords of waste" that have battled for my affections: _____, _____, _____, _____, _____, and _____ (control, regret, fear, and busyness). These have caused much pain, disintegrated my heart, and weakened my affections for Christ.

By the power of the gospel and the Holy Spirit I have begun to practice gospel repentance by _____, receive gospel healing for _____, and I am trusting the gospel by taking risks in the following areas: _____

_____

_____.

I am beginning to practice each day the spiritual disciplines of solitude (silence, word, and prayer with God), embracing the sorrow for unmet longings, dream disillusionment, and spiritual discernment of God's will. He is forming integrity and congruity from the inside out through gospel healing. God is healing my relationships by differentiating me from others and by keeping me present to my family, church, workplace, and community.

Having understood God's four-part story and applied it to my own in four chapters, He has revealed gospel themes in each chapter that seem to converge in midlife, which are _____
_____
_____.

My Eden (chapter 1) and experience of Shalom that came to mind from my youth was _____
_____.

The fall (chapter 2) and the shattering of shalom came in three categories:

I was "orphaned" without support and guidance when _____
_____.

I was "alienated" when I was _____
_____.

I was "widowed" (heart crushed in romance) when I was _____
_____.

My chapter of *redemption* (chapter 3) can be felt by the times when _____
_____
_____.

I can imagine the final chapter of *consummation* (chapter 4) when I come into heaven to see Christ in all His glory, while I am glorified into His likeness. I trust He will, in some way, take something of the substance of my Eden chapter and will make all things new in the final chapter. I am intentionally running again towards that day.

Therefore, by engaging in the battle for my affections, I seek to defeat the warlords of waste; by gospel repentance I am experiencing joy and freedom to make choices; by the Spirit's healing and reintegrating my heart I am declaring independence from the rule of painful events and others; by differentiating from relationships of enmeshment I am staying more warmly present to my community; and by raising a convergence of my experience and God's grace to me, I want to live with intentionality for Christ in the following ways:

1. In the next year, I choose to go to war against the following "mighty warlords of midlife" and idols of my heart to the death.

2. In the next year, I choose to make the spiritual disciplines of solitude (silence, word, meditation, embracing sorrow, disillusionment, and discernment) a daily habit of the heart.

   When?
   How?
   Why?

3. In the next 5–10 years, I choose to live with intentionality for Christ to cultivate gospel transformation among my:

   Family:
   Marriage:
   Children:
   Grandchildren:
   Parents:
   Siblings:
   Friends:
   Church:
   Workplace:

Locally Community:
Globally:

4. In this next decade, I choose to live with gospel intentionality for Christ with regard to:

Diet:
Exercise:
Assets:
Debts:
New Efforts:

I am becoming more solid about my identity in Christ, more secure about my place and calling to Christ, and I want to live with intentionality for Christ until I receive from Him a legacy worth giving to the next generation.

Conclusion

What is the Next Season of Spiritual Formation?

We have covered a lot of material with regard to reigniting our affections and intentionality for Christ. It is a process, a season, and you have taken the first step. Over the years God will clarify this season of spiritual formation as you reread and reapply the material to your life.

This book has defined the Christian's intentionality for Christ, offered gospel motivation in intentionality, addressed four mighty warlords of waste that battle for our affections, assisted in the interpretation process of your story, sought to see the convergence of your experience and God's grace to you, and helped to personalize your intentions for Christ by providing a template for you to write out and share with others.

The key question in this season of spiritual formation is: What's my aim? John Calvin has a nice paragraph about the importance of aim. He wrote:

> What then? Let us set this before our eye as the end at which we ought constantly to aim. Let it be regarded as the goal towards which we are to run. For you cannot divide the matter with God,

undertaking part of what his word enjoins, and omitting part at pleasure. For, in the first place, God uniformly recommends integrity as the principal part of his worship, meaning by integrity real singleness of mind, devoid of gloss and fiction, and to this is opposed a double mind; as if it had been said, that the spiritual commencement of a good life is when the internal affections are sincerely devoted to God, in the cultivation of holiness and justice. But seeing that, in this earthly prison of the body, no man is supplied with strength sufficient to hasten in his course with due alacrity, while the greater number are so oppressed with weakness, that hesitating, and halting, and even crawling on the ground, they make little progress, let every one of us go as far as his humble ability enables him, and prosecute the journey once begun. No one will travel so badly as not daily to make some degree of progress.[58]

I would encourage you to participate in the whole series of Four Spiritual Seasons of Spiritual Formation—Identity in Christ, Calling to Christ, Intentionality for Christ, and Legacy from Christ. These four books are designed to shape you into a godly Christian who takes the fourfold seasons of the Christian life to heart.

The next two books are forthcoming under the same publisher, and you may benefit as well by going to my blog at http://www.identityinchrist.com

Please contact me for speaking or for help along the way.

---

[58] John Calvin, *Institutes of the Christian Religion* (Philadelphia, PA: The Westminster Press, 1960), Book 3. Chapter 6. Section 3, Volume One, pp. 688–689.

Bibliography

Dan Allender, https://theallendercenter.org/2015/05/endings-4/

_____, Dan Allender and Tremper Longman III, *The Cry of The Soul: How Our Emotions Reveal Our Deepest Questions About God* (Colorado Springs, CO: Navpress, 1994).

_____, *To Be Told: Know Your Story, Shape Your Life* (Colorado Springs, CO: WaterBrook Press, 2005).

Dietrich Bonhoeffer, *The Cost of Discipleship* (New York, NY: Macmillan, 1963, repr. 1979).

John Calvin, *Commentary on A Harmony of the Evangelists, Matthew, Mark, and Luke* (Grand Rapids, MI: Baker Book House, reprint 1993), Volume 27.

Oswald Chambers, *My Utmost for His Highest: Selections for the Year* (New York, NY: Dodd, Mead & Company, 1935, repr. 1959).

Gilbert K. Chesterton, *Orthodoxy* (New York, NY: John Lane Company, 1908).

Larry Crabb, *Shattered Dreams: God's Unexpected Pathway to Joy* (Colorado Springs, CO: WaterBrook Press, 2001) .

Jonathan Edwards, *The Works of Jonathan Edwards* (New Haven, MA: Yale University Press, 1959), Volume 2.

_____, *The Works of Jonathan Edwards* (New Haven, CT: Yale University Press, 1992),Volume 10.

_____, *The Works of Jonathan Edwards* (New Haven, CT: Yale University Press, 1997),Volume 14.

_____, *The Works of Jonathan Edwards* (New Haven, CT: Yale University Press, 1998),Volume 16.

Daniel Fuller, *The Unity of the Bible: Unfolding God's Plan for Humanity* (Grand Rapids, Mich.: Zondervan, 1992).

Howard Hendricks, *Teaching to Change Lives: Seven Proven Ways to Make Your Teaching Come Alive* (Sisters, OR: Multnomah Publishers, 1987).

Matthew Henry, *Matthew Henry's Commentary* (Col 3:5–8).

Timothy J. Keller, *Counterfeit Gods: The Empty Promise of Money, Sex, and Power and the Only Hope that Matters* (New York, NY: Dutton, 2009).

John Lenin and Paul McCartney, "Nowhere Man" in *Rubber Soul* album (Abbey Road Studios: EMI Records, October 12, 1965), The Beatles.

George Eldon Ladd, *The Gospel of the Kingdom: Scriptural Studies in the Kingdom of God* (Grand Rapids, MI: Eerdmans Publishing, 1959).

C. S. Lewis, *The Screwtape Letters* (New York, NY: HarperCollins, 1987).

David Martin Lloyd Jones, *Spiritual Depression: Its Causes and Cures* (London, UK: HarperCollins, 1965, repr. 1998).

Herman Mellville, *Redburn*, (Chicago, IL: Northwestern University Press, 1969, repr. 1993).

Albert Mohler, http://www.albertmohler.com/2016/08/12/god-made-china-eric-liddell-beyond-olympic-glory/

Henri J. M. Nouwen, *The Wounded Healer: Ministry in Contemporary Society* (New York, NY: Doubleday, 1972, repr. 1990).

_____, *Life of the Beloved: Spiritual Living in a Secular World* (Wheaton, IL: Crossway Books, 2007), p. 35. Kindle Edition.

_____, *The Return of the Prodigal Son*, (New York, NY: Penguin Random House, 1992).

_____, *With Open Hands* (Notre Dame, IN: Ave Maria Press, 1972, repr. 2006).

_____, *The Wounded Healer: Ministry in Contemporary Society* (New York, NY: Doubleday, 1972).

Andrew Peterson, "Planting Trees" in *Counting Stars* album released through Centricity Music on July 27, 2010.

Eugene H. Peterson, *A Long Obedience in the Same Direction* (Downers Grove, IL: InterVarsity Press, 1980).

John Piper, *Don't Waste Your Life* (Wheaton, IL: Crossway Books, 2007).

Rebecca Pippert, *Out of the Saltshaker* (Downers Grove, Il.: InterVarsity Press, 1979).

Neil Postman, *Amusing Ourselves to Death: Public Discourse in the Age of Show Business* (New York, NY: Penguin Books, 1985).

Robert Davis Smart, *Embracing Your Identity in Christ: Renouncing Lies and Foolish Strategies* (Bloomington, IN: Westbow Press, 2017).

_____, *Calling to Christ: Where's My Place?* (Bloomington, IN: WestBow Press, 2017).

_____, *Legacy from Christ: What's My Message?* (Bloomington, IN: WestBow Press, 2017).

Charles H. Spurgeon, "Repentance after Conversion," Sermon, No. 2419, June 12, 1887.

Richard A. Swenson, *Margin: Restoring Emotional, Physical, Financial, and Time Reserves to Overloaded Lives* (Colorado Springs, CO: Navpress, 2004) Kindle Edition.

Paul David Tripp, *Lost in the Middle—MidLife and the Grace of God* (Wapwallopen, PA: Shepherd Press, 2004).

Ella Wheeler Wilcox, "The Winds of Fate" in *World Voices* (New York, NY: Hearst's International Library Company, 1916).

Appendix
Seasons One and Two Templates

My Identity in Christ

Note: This template is from the first season of spiritual formation. You may want to write it out again, or skip to the intentionality template.

My name is _____ (full name). I am the son of _____, the grandson of _____ and _____ (give brief explanation). I am the husband/wife of _____ and the father/mother of _____.

I am made in the image of God, which means I am _____. I am a fallen image bearer too, and therefore a "glorious ruin." I am a man/woman, and not a woman/man, which means my glory as a man/woman is expressed by _____. I am a broken man/woman, which means the curse in Genesis 3 was meant to make me long for another Man (Jesus) to save and change me into His likeness. My brokenness is seen in the way I _____.

I renounce my core lie and Satan's condemning thought that I am _____, and I renounce my foolish and autonomous strategies to overcome this lie—also my surrender to this lie from time to time. These foolish strategies, which did and do not work, are _____

_____ .

I am pardoned of all my sins and declared righteous in God's sight, but only for the righteousness of Christ imputed to me and received by faith alone, which means I am justified.

I am the son of God the Father, who chose me in love to be adopted into his family through Jesus. And I cry out for intimacy with him through the Holy Spirit; saying, "Abba! Father!"

I am a saint, a holy one, a consecrated man/woman for holiness of life and calling. I am anointed with the Holy Spirit and gifted with spiritual gifts of love, power, and effective service in all of life and every relationship. I am a new creature in Christ, and declare war with my old, sinful nature in the irreconcilable war that lasts until heaven (definitively sanctified).

My Calling to Christ

Note: This template is from the second season of spiritual formation. You may want to write it out again, or skip to the intentionality template.

My calling to Christ flows out of my identity in Christ as His workmanship. I am His workmanship created in Christ to do good works predestined for me. God called me first and foremost to Christ, who clarifies my calling as a _____,

_____, _____, etc.

My calling is unique and meaningful in my principal works of _____ and peripheral works like _____.

I am taking down and removing by the power of the gospel the following hindrances to hearing my calling to Christ such as _____

_____ .

God is using the kairotic events in my life to direct me to fulfill His call on my life—both the tragedies and redemptive ones.

What makes me weep is _____, because I love mercy.

What makes me angry is _____, because I act justly.

What I love to do is _____, as I walk humbly before God. (Micah 6:8)

The gospel oracle in this season of my life, like mail to be delivered, is _____

_____.

God is calling me to capture His vision for leading with vision (as a king), which calls me to disrupt foolish behavior (as a prophet) and invite others to gospel transformation (as a priest) in order to call them out into a glorious future.

He has called me to this place, where I am finding contentment in knowing that He not only knows what is best for His Kingdom and my calling, but also He knows how to contact me for a calling to another place or particular calling.

Notes

Notes

Notes

Notes

Notes

Notes

Notes

Notes

Notes

Notes

Notes

Made in the USA
Monee, IL
21 September 2022